BY THE SAME AUTHOR

1981 *Music for the Oberufer Christmas Plays*
1982 *Weft for the Rainbow* (Poems for classroom recitation)
1987 *The Waldorf Song Book*
1989 *Meteor Showers and Us* (Poems for classroom recitation)
1990 *A Round of Rounds*
1991 *Becoming a Steiner School*
1992 *Patter-Paws the Fox* (A class reader)
1993 *The Second Waldorf Song Book*
1993 *Waldorf Curriculum Studies: Science* (Ed.)
1995 *Concordance: Rudolf Steiner / Waldorf Education*
1997 *An Appraisal of Steinerian Theory and Waldorf Praxis:*
How do they compare?
1998 *Trumpets of Happiness* (A class reader)
1998 *Owen Barfield: A Waldorf Tribute* (Ed.)
2000 *Index: Child and Man / Steiner Education 1977–2000*

D1331940

ADVENTURES IN
STEINER EDUCATION

ADVENTURES IN STEINER EDUCATION

AN INTRODUCTION TO THE WALDORF APPROACH

BRIEN MASTERS

Sophia Books

Sophia Books
Hillside House, The Square
Forest Row, East Sussex
RH18 5ES

Published by Sophia Books 2005
An imprint of Rudolf Steiner Press

A catalogue record for this book is available from the British Library

ISBN 1 85584 153 3

Cover by Andrew Morgan Design based on photographs by
Judith Brown (Kenya) and Ligita Gaile (Latvia)
Typeset by DP Photosetting, Aylesbury, Bucks.
Printed and bound in Great Britain by Cromwell Press Limited,
Trowbridge, Wilts.

To
All those Colleagues
—on both sides of the 'threshold'—
with whom I have so often sat at the
Round Table of Collegiality
without whom these
'Adventures' in Steiner Education
would have been no more than a
Lone Knight
Questing in a Hostile World

Contents

Acknowledgements

In the South Transept of Chartres Cathedral in Northern France the medieval stained glass artist has left us a powerful image of the four Evangelists, sitting on the shoulders of Old Testament prophets. Ample food for thought, indeed. Not at all implying any hint of superiority, however. In fact the prophets are depicted as being much grander in style. Nevertheless the image is an acknowledgement of indebtedness. In naming those to whom I am beholden in regard to this present work, I am distinctly aware of sitting on the shoulders, as it were, of three generations.

Rudolf Steiner stands there in the past, as the source of the education here described. Much as a mountain spring rises in rare, precipitous heights, far upstream from the mouth of a vast, navigable river—energy-giving waters that surfaced in the past—his inspiration remains ever present in the deep, vital and never failing currents that flow via his spiritual insight into the ocean of life.

Another potent source of inspiration has been those whose brief words are recorded anonymously at the beginning of each chapter. These have been mostly the younger generation, contact with whom in professional, domestic and other circumstances it has been my privilege to enjoy. They are, of course, only a tiny handful of the hosts of children of all ages that have been sources of stimulation in dozens of different teaching and life situations. Although some of them are by now joining the ranks of 'senior citizens', I think of them—and pin my hope on them, as would any teacher—as the future generation.

My contemporaries, also too numerous to name one by one, are those who have been colleagues. The book's dedication is my attempt to express my lasting debt of gratitude to them. As to the lecturing, teacher training and advising in which I have been engaged for the past quarter of a century, my thoughts turn with sincere appreciation to the instigators, organizers, financiers and kind hosts of such sorties, those in the UK as much as those abroad.

In trying to encompass so many in my mind, I am reminded of the patient at a home for the mentally handicapped who, being taken to the theatre, mistakenly picked up the telephone directory instead of a programme. Not knowing this, the supervisor half glanced over her shoulder to ask him if he had finished reading the programme notes. 'I haven't got there yet', he replied laconically, 'but what a cast!'

I also wish to include a special word of thanks to Sevak Gulbekian of Sophia Books, who commissioned this work. Having read what I submitted by way of a sample chapter, after some discussion he recommended that I adopt a less academic style, drawing on my personal experiences as the main thrust of the book, and letting the rich panorama of Waldorf unfold from those. Following his advice has not only been a pleasure, it has heightened my realization of just how much we owe to those personal meetings, those paths that cross, and those windows that open, throughout life.

Finally a deep word of thanks to my wife and family, who recently have sympathized with my consternation at the loss of electronic documents and the like, and borne the brunt of my lateness for meals during those last (very elastic) 'five minutes' of spell-checking; and who, over the years, have always been ready to hear the repeated animation with which I returned from the adventures here glimpsed at, with welcome ears and with composure, having held the domestic fort during my sometimes lengthy absences.

Preface

The harvest of books on Steiner (or Waldorf) education is becoming increasingly abundant. Fortunately they are not as numerous as the memoirs of politicians, but there is a similarity in that they are written mostly when active participation is receding into the past. However, with few exceptions (Torin Finser's *School as a Journey* and Hermann Koepke's *Encountering the Self*) literature arising from the practitioner's direct experience tends to be confined to Waldorf journals and school magazines which reach a comparatively limited public. Consequently, the following chapters are an attempt to present the education in a way that draws on personal experiences while at the same time, through reflecting on those experiences, achieving a cohesive overview.

The classroom is notorious as a place where things move fast. Those fast moving memories of the teacher are like the minute hand of a clock. Once one has left the lesson the second and minute hands are no longer dizzily turning. Nevertheless, unless one's head has become ostrich-like, buried in the sand, one remains aware of the hour hand's movement through observing the changes in education generally.

Staying with friends in the 30s, I recall visiting a country school for a few days where we wrote on slates. I can still feel the cool smoothness of the writing implement we used, stroking the skin between my thumb and index finger. A far cry it was from today's word processing. The hour hand of the teaching profession includes such sequences of teaching styles as encapsulated in the terms *blackboard, chalk board, wipe board*. Even the movement of the hour hand—or should it be hour *digits*?—is becoming visible in the current scene as the exterior appearance of education jerks along, in a frequently market-driven attempt to keep up with the Jones's rapid electronic escalations. Personally, I am content to think of myself as having spent my teaching career at the *chalk face*, rather than at the *wipe face*!

But this is to get stuck on the surface of things. And if one remains there, instead of digging below and examining the roots, superficiality will inevitably prevail. Indeed, might the rapid changes we experience in various spheres of life, not only in education, indicate the merest of shallow roots, or worse: shallowness and ephemera in the extreme? And the noisy public debates that go on having the effect of desensitizing our awareness and judgements?

There is something healthy about change. Not change for change's sake, of course, the stuff of politics etc. Devoid of change we would feel rutted in anachronisms. Yet we often condone inconsistencies. Teaching in the 50s, I don't recall feeling like a blot on the contemporary landscape as I stood before the up and coming generation wearing my academic gown. By comparison with such a lingering medieval tradition—and there are others—Steiner education stands out a mile as a very new boy, without a single scuff on his boots or a single blemish on his newly starched shirt collar. However, we questioningly raise our eyebrows—and rightly so—when we realize that in Steiner there is a whole 'method' that stems from the year 1919. While we appreciate good track records, we also expect *development*. Indeed, these days there can hardly be staff without a staff development programme, or a curriculum without a curriculum development plan... Where then, we may ask, is the vibrancy of the here and now to be found in Steiner?

A July 2004 graduate of the London Waldorf Teacher Training Seminar had been doing a Post Graduate Certificate of Education (PGCE) in parallel with the seminar. He commented on the unexpectedly infrequent references to children per se made by his lecturers on the PGCE. Thus: going through such a higher educational hoop, it is considered professional to acquire a state teaching qualification with little 'formal' knowledge of children! This is where Steiner excelled. If one thinks of the four main components of standard education theory—(i) aims, (ii) the nature of the child, (iii) curriculum, (iv) pedagogy—he placed an unprecedented emphasis on the nature of the child and on (thumbs up, the establishment!) child *development!* Therefore, for anyone wishing to extrapolate Steiner's theory of education from his vast output on the subject, they will be at sea unless they realize that he virtually subordinated the other three components to the nature and development of children. Even *aims*, one might argue, were seen partly as the outcome of the child *when become adult*, an adult whose self-directing driving force in life was a major determinant in fashioning the future.

One aim that most educationalists would probably be content to agree with would be to produce a 'good citizen'. If that were the only banner there would be a long procession tramping after it. But itemize what constitutes a good citizen and the apparent solidarity would quickly splinter. I will refrain from hypothesizing as to what Steiner's version of a good citizen would have been—and in any case it would certainly have prompted a lengthy course of lectures!—but one could assume with certainty that it would focus on the inner qualities of the adult that had been there as a potential through childhood, and nurtured through education, until they bore fruit as a *positive contribution to society and to the earth as the stage upon which human life is enacted, as well as to the person's own biography.*

Put like that it sounds rather grandiose. Nothing presumptuous is remotely intended, however. The most positive of lives can go on well behind the scenes of publicity—even concealed behind a veil of complete anonymity—but nevertheless be of inestimable value in evolution and entirely meaningful for the individual.

But to return to so-called education theory and the fact that Steiner saw both the curriculum and the *how* of teaching it as evolving directly from an understanding of the nature of the child. For the teacher to be the active force in this (rather than something deriving from an Act of Parliament), she cannot rely on it all being 'in the book'. Although all children do have something in common with the universal pattern of human development, each one in the class also incorporates a unique individuality—Marie Curie, Nelson Mandela, Hildegard of Bingen, The Unknown Warrior, Mary Mary quite Contrary . . . This places the onus to be fast-moving, germane and contemporary not on a system that was inaugurated in August 1919 but on the teacher in the classroom this very day. No wonder Steiner also gave helpful advice for the inner life, so that teacher development was not only a matter of keeping abreast with outer circumstances. Without that advice and the professional attitude of the teacher who incorporates it in some form or other into her daily practice, Steiner education could never have evolved into the World Movement that it has become—become, moreover, despite many setbacks.

One sometimes wonders what happens to the volumes of 'paper work' churned out by teachers in many 'conventional' systems of education. If public reports and the press are anything to go by, the resultant demand made on teachers' time is not only a political football, it is an acute professional problem. The boot could be described as being on the other foot with the Waldorf teacher. She is so busy teaching—and the whole ethic of preparation and collegial consultation that goes with it—that her teaching experience seldom filters through to the printed page. It is therefore with a feeling of thankfulness that destiny has presented me with the time to step away from the chalk face and, somewhat in memoir fashion, investigate the roots of which the incidents described in the following chapters are clearly blossoms, scattered over the years. At the same time, I trust that the final result will not only give the reader intimate access to the nuances of events that occurred long after 1919, but also a fair impression of the bounteous and inviting landscape of Steiner education per se.

Brien Masters
Easter 2005

PREVIEW

Between Zeal and Scepticism

'What in heaven's name is a reading age?'

It came like a dart of lightning, quivering imperceptibly for a moment whilst the rest of us took some seconds to regain our breath.

The occasion was a public relations exercise staged by a go-ahead group of parents and teachers from the newly born Rudolf Steiner School of South Devon. A huge marquee had been erected in a field. From the neighbouring farms the faint but distinctive smells of milk, manure and lush grass being munched hung in the air. The Steiner education workshop had got to the point where the introductory talk had led over into discussion. Formalities had been discarded. Babes in arms abounded as did babes not in arms (one with a dummy at one end and a fat, damp nappy trailing at the other, wagging with inquisitiveness while approaching the shoelaces of the guest speaker!). Participants sat around under the shelter of the canvas, clutching their cartons of steaming soup or home-made elder-flower pressé. They voiced their concerns, their lingering doubts, their need for reassurance that this was an education for real, not just sheltered workshops for the 'special needs' cases with which they vaguely, if with admiration, connected the name of Steiner.

How to pitch what you have to say on such an occasion is always a sensitive issue. The organizers are reaching out to a cross-section of society that might not otherwise stumble across Steiner education—people who wouldn't be likely to turn out for an evening lecture in the local Town Hall, still less in the school itself. But here, amongst the straw bales, anyone could feel at home. Family familiarity pervaded the air, children looking like children were blowing bubbles, wafting coloured windmills in figures of eight, needing their noses wiped at intervals, dangling balloons, doing cartwheels, licking toffee apples, wearing necklaces of buttercup chains— all in country fayre fashion. Yet behind the decided twinkle in the social eye was the very focused *aim*: attract parents and thus their children to our new school. This guarantees quite a cocktail of an audience. There are the newcomers, curious, genuinely interested, cynical (dragged there by their partners, maybe), *and* the preaching-to-the-converted old hands—not to mention the outspokenly zealous, as the incident cited above well demonstrates. All mingling affably enough.

The old hands well know why they've chosen Steiner, and are prepared to fork out financial support from a hard-earned income for the sake of their growing child's education.

Some reasons parents are attracted to Waldorf

● Parents had been up in arms about the pressure of formal early learning. But their hearts immediately went out when they first witnessed the gentle atmosphere of the Steiner Kindergarten, where children have, on the one hand, the structured day which is so essential for their development and, on the other hand, time to play, to be children, to learn 'experientially', to freely exercise those growing limbs, to drink in delicate and natural sense impressions.

● These parents have themselves been thoroughly ground by the mill of an exam-saturated educational system, which is why they have searched high and low for an approach that gives space for the developing child to find and give expression to his or her own individuality.

● They have had to cope with intellectually orientated syl-labuses. But they have since come to recognize the value of Steiner's holistic approach, which gives vent to the child's otherwise stultified emotional intelligence.

• Having suffered from being hard driven intellectually at an early age, they had then been forced into the confines of a few A levels. But now, they have come to recognize the value of all pupils in Steiner schools being led into ever wider horizons of knowledge and experience, through taking a broad range of subjects in the sciences, arts and humanities— not to mention movement education and the wealth of crafts which the school provides.

• They have unpleasantly lingering memories of their own schools as places where they suspect they had counted for little more than a number on the roll—potential exam fodder, a valuable contribution to (or, as the case may be, a threat to) the school's position in the league tables—rather than as a person in their own right. But since then they have been attracted by the empathy and care they found in the Steiner ethos, both amongst staff (not a head teacher but a faculty that carries mutual responsibility for the school's affairs) and parents, as well as pupils—the kind of care that values the worth of each individual.

• They had left school with a B in French, say, but soon discovered the inadequacy of the system on finding that they were unable to hold even an elementary conversation with the first Frenchman they met on landing in Paris. So they were impressed by Steiner's conversational approach to languages and the corresponding truly international dimension of the Steiner movement—with nigh on 1000 schools and twice as many Kindergartens all working from the same educational philosophy in 53 different countries across all five continents and in a colourful variety of cultural settings.

• They only too readily recall the bitter taste of 'failure' as a result of the incessant emphasis on percentages, attainment targets, position in class and so on. Hence resignation, the all too familiar syndrome: Why bother? But since, they have become heartened by the Steiner method of assessment:

lengthy, descriptive end–of–year reports which are free of the dreaded 'could–do–better' clichés, with teachers additionally often speaking to parents, and home visits (teachers' telephone numbers are published in the school's newsletter to facilitate parents being kept in the picture so that any incipient problems can be nipped in the bud).

• Their heart sinks even now at the thought of the low morale they experienced way back in their school days as a result of lesson after lesson that was simply not inspiring. This applied not only to the teaching of the sciences, which as recent surveys show is still very much in the dock, or to maths lessons (they clearly remember peers who developed something of a phobia for the subject). But they have come to relish the babble at the supper table as their children at the Steiner school enthuse over the various things they have been doing in class.

• They remember feeling particularly forlorn when, after only one year, they had to leave a teacher who was one of the few bright spots in a long week. So they have become won over to the class teacher system in Steiner schools in which one teacher remains with his or her class for most subjects over a period of six to eight years, thus providing the stability that is such a large factor in how children make progress. (That of course depends nowadays on whether the law of the particular country allows the original eight–year stretch to run its full course.)

• Their abiding memories of school may have been of barrack–like, drab surroundings. In contrast they have been watching their own children blossom as they come into the colourful and aesthetic environment of a Steiner school.

• Through having children of their own, their memories will have been sparked off of the long hours of boredom through which certain lessons plodded, and the reluctance with which they dragged themselves out of the front door on days when these lessons were scheduled. They then marvel to see how their child at the Steiner school cheerily goes off to catch the school minibus, looking forward to what the day may hold in store.

● In several cases parents have taken up the teaching profession themselves—despite having vowed never to do so—and become increasingly disillusioned as 'the system' tightens its stranglehold. But they have since come to recognize, through professional insight, how the creative approach that teachers enjoy in the Steiner setting is beneficial both for the teacher and the children.

● The parents had felt browbeaten by their elders with the ominous 'when you're grown up . . .' but only realized on hindsight that the kind of linear thinking it encompassed applied more to the machine world than to a growing child. Now they have become inspired to look anew at human development through Steiner's concept of the great transformations that take place at different stages of childhood, resulting in the learning emphasis starting with *activity* and only shifting to a *rational mode of thinking* via a vividly *imaginative* phase in the middle years.

● They have become frustrated by the all too frequent changes that successive governments introduce, with their 'Old Mother Hubbard' cupboard, barren of inspiration—frustration that is compounded by resentfulness at feeling let down just at important turning points in their own school careers. For they have come to appreciate the significant continuity value of the 85-year track record of Steiner education, and warm to its basic philosophy, brimful of ideas, but nevertheless *non-prescriptive* and therefore easily adaptable to this or that setting.

● They inwardly groan as they think back to their own school days when Oliver Cromwell cropped up for the third year running in the syllabus. Or, if they are grandparents, they remember the long hours spent over the parsing of sentences, or stuff that seemed of very limited use ('When,' wondered the young and notoriously non-academic Winston Churchill, 'am I going to need to say *in Latin*: "O thou table . . ."?!'). Subsequently they have become impressed—as were Steiner's contemporaries—by the sharp cutting edge of the Steiner curriculum, particularly at secondary level, and the willingness of teachers to discuss issues which the young people find particularly relevant to their lives and aspirations, possible in the textbook-free zone of a Steiner classroom.

● They relive the relief and feeling of liberation with which they burned their school exercise books on going to university—the careless smudges, the adolescent graffiti, the disinterested scrawls and doodlings, the tatty covers, the grey outlines of embryos in test tubes, the loathed red ink, the gullibility by which they were induced to gain a 'gold star', the nausea of the tests, the corners of pages torn off for scribbling surreptitious notes to some 'partner in crime' at the other end of the row . . . all gone up in smoke and flames. The distaste and embarrassment of the past are now no more than flakes of charcoal. On the other hand they are amazed at the artistically presented work their children display at parents' evenings—the exercise books they have themselves made, illustrated and compiled, the enormous range of craft work, paintings and drawings—fancy-free in scope yet such a hallmark of the Steiner approach.

● These people will have awoken to the disjointed effect on their children's world outlook if lessons are arbitrarily chopped and changed about every 40 minutes of the day, and perhaps they associate the practice with the abstract, humanly disconnected, exclusively self-interested, at times brutally critical and analytical attitudes to life they encounter in the media and elsewhere. They have come to realize the value of the main-lesson at the beginning of each day, allowing an integrated view of life to unfold because of its generous two-hour length and month's duration.

● They have been looking for answers to the escalating problems in which society is embroiled: crime at the personal level, the use of increasingly sophisticated weapons of war and the threat of mass destruction at the global level, and the insidious wielding of economic power by so-called democracies while the needy throughout the world are herded into ever more ensnared states of impoverishment. They see in Steiner's world outlook, and the place that education holds in it, not a quick fix but at least some hope that could filter into the several branches of society through forthcoming generations.

● Perhaps above all they are impressed by the articulate way of speaking displayed by the graduates they have met from Steiner schools, their psychological stamina, their confidence in the meaning of life, their wide range of interests, their positivity, their ease in a variety of social settings, their flexibility, and the fulfilment they derive from the grass *this* side of the fence though at the same time not being blind to the needs of the wider community.

These snippets gathered from remarks made by parents who have chosen Steiner education for their children are, of course, not intended to imply that the aims of the education are always fully realized. Such a claim would go too far. They *do*, however, illustrate the sort of thing that has tipped the scales when those parents have come to weigh up in their lives which way to go regarding their children's education.

So much for the 'converted'.

The newcomers, by contrast, those who are hearing of Steiner for the first time, little realize initially that an elaborate philosophy underpins the life in the classroom. They do not know that behind the Welsh tune being played on recorders first thing in the morning, or the Spanish poem being recited in chorus, or the flurry of mental arithmetic, or the symmetry drawings on the pin-board, or the class exchange with a school abroad, or the time devoted to a drama production midst the A level exam year, or the unusual branches of mathematics that are pursued with such gusto (such as Platonic solids at age 14, or projective geometry three years later), or indeed that behind all that goes on within and without the walls of a Steiner school there is a wealth of thought that makes this approach to education a unique one.

Moreover, the newcomers probably little realize that Rudolf Steiner (1861–1925), the inaugurator and co-founder of the school movement, was also remarkably informed about a host of other fields: medicine, nutrition, agriculture, astronomy, psychology, architecture and drama, to mention some. They may little realize—and might be tempted to think twice if they did—that behind the eye-catching leaflet on display at the entrance to the marquee, and the well-illustrated school prospectus, is a library door key which gives access to numerous published books and printed transcripts of some 6000 lectures Steiner gave, all in a comparatively short span of time, not to mention the impressive amount of secondary literature.

On thinking twice, however, especially in an age where lifelong learning is a watchword, they soon realize that, without a firm rationale, constantly exposed to the rigour of modern thought, an education in which *children enjoy school* could easily become suspect. While the heart is frequently starved in modern life, nourishing it should clearly not be a licence for neglecting the mind. Far from it. After all, it is the *whole* child that education ideally should be about. Indeed, one might say that it is the very nature of what constitutes the 'whole child' that summarizes Steiner's main concerns and provided him with a starting point.

Some of the greatest hurdles newcomers to Steiner education will have to negotiate are current modes of thought—hardly *thought*, even—which have become ingrained and therefore unchallenged in society. When someone comes along and questions a financially hugely successful 'institution' such as Disney Land—as the Archbishop of Canterbury did on his appointment in the late summer of 2002—it is not surprising that people quickly take up defensive attitudes. We're understandably not comfortable with the ground shaking beneath our feet. Wouldn't it be the same if someone questioned the validity of video games for children or the fetish that has built up around sport? But until someone does the necessary thinking, and has the necessary guts to make their conclusions known, it is all too easy for the rest of us to stay within the ranks of those who timidly approve 'the emperor's new clothes', despite his self-evident nudity—and maybe his somewhat repulsive ugliness, his atrocious contempt of humanity and his obscene flaunting of wealth.

On the subject of literacy, it seems almost heretical to question what after all has been a fairly straight line of development ever since Gutenberg and Caxton started their printing activities all those centuries ago. But Steiner's is no longer a lone voice in bringing a new approach to this field, nor has it by any means been his only innovation. And that is what the woman at the workshop in the marquee on that showery summer day burst out with, totally frustrated with what to her was the niggling, myopic persistence of the newcomer who would take nothing less than a reasoned, cogent and lucid reply for an answer.

When I wrote the following chapters, they were prompted by the notion that the zealot would perhaps benefit from as much cogency and lucidity as would the sceptic—why not?—not to mention those whose spectrum of thought lies somewhere in between the two polarities.

The Waldorf Approach to Literacy

Expert Explodes Learning Myth.

That was the headline in the morning press in Armidale, Australia, the day after I'd given a public lecture on Steiner education in which I'd been asked to highlight the Waldorf approach to literacy. You have to hand it to journalism! What academic could have come up with a four-word sentence that is at once so attention riveting while telling you absolutely nothing till you read the ensuing article?

While not having any truck with 'reading ages', as with the case of the parent quoted in the previous chapter, we are touching here on one of Steiner's main sticking points, which over the years has come to distinguish Waldorf education increasingly from the trend found in many forms of State education. The local Stuttgart authorities in 1919 required that the pupils from the Waldorf School be on a par with those in State schools by the time they had completed the third class. While the Waldorf curriculum as envisaged by Steiner was considerably in advance of the State system in several respects, when it came to literacy he saw the required parity as a significant obstacle. The compromise Steiner settled for was the well-known Waldorf method of leading the pupils into literacy. This entailed definite stages. The main ones are: writing introduced well before reading; capitals well in place before the introduction of 'small' letters; the appropriate use of narrative combined with imagery; the sound, the shape and the 'name' of the letter introduced simultaneously.

This method has been described, analysed and revisited time and again. Its main stumbling block for parents is the *social* effect its contrast with the usual system presents. For instance, two children aged 7 can be playing together at home, with the Waldorf pupil having just embarked on the above process while the neighbour's child has already been reading for two or three years. Whilst children usually take such things in their stride or are simply oblivious to them and are only too happy to have a friend with whom they can engage, adults may take a different view. They may be otherwise well-meaning neighbours, relatives or even shopkeepers. They drop comments which, while not being crassly supercilious, may nevertheless irritate. If they are going to stand their ground and fend off any negative repercussions of such remarks, it is therefore necessary for Waldorf parents to be aware that the method in all its aspects is one of the keystones of Waldorf—essentially a non-negotiable *maxim*.

It frequently happens on part-time Waldorf teacher training courses that teachers from the State system are attracted by Steiner's enriching and productive ideas, the constraints with which the State requires them to operate notwithstanding. A deputy head teacher from a multi-ethnic London borough was in that situation. He decided to import one or two elements from Steiner's approach to literacy into the classroom. Despite many of his 6/7-year-olds being 'nursery-slope' readers (upper *and* lower case) they took to the approach—especially the *pictorial* element. He had chosen to teach the letter 'M', starting by telling a story of a mountain with twin peaks. The next day he had the children drawing pictures of the story, the central feature of which was a large A4-size mountain with steep sloping sides. As he circulated, praising, commenting and giving encouragement, he came to one drawing which had a decided lump at the foot of the right-hand mountain slope. 'What is that, Hugh?' he asked, pointing to the lump. 'Oh,' replied the boy with delight, 'that's a little mountain,' (and he traced an 'h' over it with his index finger) ' "h"—it stands for "hill"!' The method had liberated the child's pictorial fantasy even though intellectually he had already 'been there' for some time.

One should not assume, however, that Steiner, despite the value he attached to the method, would have recommended introducing anything and everything in a pictorial way. We shall return to this particularly in connection with numeracy. Why he was so emphatic about the pedagogical importance of it in teaching literacy is bound up with the nature of the written word and the nature of the young child. In Steiner's view of childhood, young children are still embedded in the state of consciousness that Owen Barfield termed 'partici-pative' (see *Saving the Appearances*, Faber & Faber 1957). In the natural course of their development, they have not 'abstracted' themselves from their environment. Our immense environmental problems have become high on the agenda of contemporary issues because by and large we have lost touch with nature—a seeming paradox if one considers the enormous amount of analytical research that is taking place regarding all aspects of nature. This is not the place to go into holism, but it may suffice to say that unless the *whole* is taken into account, the conclusions that are deducted from empirical research, however precise, are not necessarily going to reliably resemble the full truth.

Therefore Steiner's solution to the problem of teaching something that he considered abstract (the *written* word) compared with its origin, the *spoken* word and the source of inspiration which informed it, was to make the method of teaching as enlivening as possible. Such a method could be said to provide a psychological counterbalance for the pupil. Or more elaborately: it lifts the letter from the dead abstract form, in which the living sound has been incarcerated, into a sphere of experience that is related to what might be called the 'creative word', a sphere in which the child is by birth-right at home.

The sound which the letter represents (in the example above, *Mmm*) is taken by the teacher as an inspirational starting point for the so-called *letter story*. This pervades the story with its *mood*. Liberally bearing in mind the *shape* of the letter, she places it in a framework in which an object whose initial letter is the one she wishes to teach—'M' as in mountain—is prominent. The plot, the characters, the scene of action, the course of events . . . all focus towards the object.

Wrapped in their participative degree of child conscious-ness, the pupils give their undivided attention to the story as the storyteller wields her art. As she conjures them into her magic circle, their vivid inner picture-making faculty con-tinuously transforms her words into images. Vast tableaux, quickly moving scenes, finely etched details, meaning-drenched gestures weave and waft through their minds, with all the picture paths along which she leads them relating to the twin mountain peaks. Then on the days following her storytelling she revives their memory-impression of the story. The whole train of events stands once again before the mind's eye, with the pupils themselves retelling the story—linking image and spoken word still enfolded in the mood of *Mmm*.

After this a process of extraction begins. First the children draw a picture. This fixes a moment in the story through the use of coloured crayon. Though the picture is freely drawn, to commit it to paper captures one particular moment—and, without being prescriptive, the teacher will direct, perhaps, that the mountain stands centre stage. The next step, similar to zoom-lensing, is to 'think away' all the other features in the picture except the mountain and its twin peaks. And so on, inwardly repeating the process if necessary until the teacher can refer to the plain 'M' and finally declare its name: *em*. Sound, shape and name are thus all derived from the creative processes through which teacher and children have travelled together.

Along with other activities, a handful of consonants is treated in this same way during the course of a main-lesson block of about four weeks. Through this experience the children associate the written language—albeit as yet represented by little more than a few capital letters—not as squiggles on paper completely at variance with their true inner nature, but as somehow connected. The method of teaching has provided the link, has represented the 'letter' of the letter as being the fallout of the 'spirit' of the letter.

To go into the introduction of vowels and lower case letters and the act of reading itself here would be to take up a lot of space with technicalities. Interested readers can follow these aspects of literacy acquisition for themselves. In practical terms the method certainly has the required result of Waldorf pupils being at no disadvantage beside their peers. Among the positive points of the method is that it bypasses what in some cases can extend to years of trauma: *learning to read*. Indeed, as a result of this method, in every Waldorf class there will be children whose way into reading simply unfolds of itself, like an automatic door opening. For them, one could say they have learnt, but not specifically been taught, to read.

Before putting the final full-stop to this chapter, allow me to return again to Armidale. At one point in the lecture, I found myself going a bit over the top in my enthusiasm for the creative power of the *spoken word*. Casting around in my mind for a good example I alighted on the word 'butterfly'. I flitted butterfly-like from one language to another, savouring French, Italian, Spanish and other butterfly sound images one after the other: *papillon, farfalla, mariposa* ... I even dared to tell the almost racist joke about the German who thumped heavily on the table when his companions had gone into ecstasy about *their* word for butterfly, and who said gruffly,

'And vot is wronk mit Schmetterlinkk?' Finally in an attempt to sip the sweetest nectar of all, I connected with my audience—or so I thought—with: '. . . And of course there's the aboriginal word for butterfly.' There was a somewhat strained silence. Only the visiting Englishman apparently had any idea what it was! But eyes sparkled appreciatively as I pronounced it: *Undilablab*—a word which through its tender sequence of phonemes, the last syllable being softly repeated like the gentle flap of a butterfly wing, seems only to have just emerged from the chrysalis of living sound, the sphere of life itself.

Life itself. Children in Waldorf schools move from Kindergarten to Lower School at age 6/7. This principle is connected with how Steiner viewed that particular stage of child development and its connection with life. We will pursue this in the next chapter.

Life Forces

'Slum Area!'

It stung my ear as I plied my way homewards on the London-Gatwick Express. Across the aisle were two Japanese tourists making for the airport. Their excited chatter at what they saw whizzing past the window, in those unmistakable, occasionally nasal singsong nuances that one affectionately associates with Japanese, contrasted appreciably with the demure conversation coming from the English commuters and other passengers. Having enjoyed the first few minutes of this I had mentally switched off and was into my newspaper. But the sudden incision 'Slum area', wrenched me out of the article I was reading. It was not just the switch from eye to ear that was arresting, however; only a couple of hours previously, something uncannily similar though in another context had occurred.

A university professor from Tokyo had brought a group of students over to Europe. They were spending three days in England: one day on and off the open top of a double-decker London bus sightseeing, another day to go to Stratford-on-Avon to see a Shakespeare play and visit the bard's birthplace, and the third back in London to hear about Waldorf education. Slightly flattering, choosing England to get an authentic taste of Waldorf, but so be it!

Before their afternoon visit to a Waldorf school, a small reception committee hosted them in Rudolf Steiner House in the centre of the city. A professional translator had been engaged. Very professional—as I paused for the translation every few sentences in my lecture, she galloped off with remarkable finesse. No wonder the excited chatter on the train journey home struck a chord. Yet in the cataract of sound, she resorted to English for a precept for which the Japanese apparently had no word: *life forces*. It took me by surprise. Understandably nothing in the modern Japanese environment that the tourists were familiar with resembled the cramped, slummy looking, smirched-brick housing of Greater London that backed onto the railway track, but surely, I thought, students of child development must have come across some such concept as 'life forces' at some point in their programme (I had carefully avoided Steiner's frequently used terminology 'etheric'). But evidently not. Nevertheless, their interest was unabated.

Steiner maintained that the physical substances of which the human body is composed were to be thought of as distinct from the life forces which informed them—indeed, totally permeated them. In embryo these life forces are already vigorously at work. Conversely, and by definition, they cease to sustain life at death. The approximately three-days' lyke wake known to the Scots, as with similar traditions in other cultures, takes place as the severed life forces are completely 'dissolving' their connection with the body.

They are forces—energies might have been a term that Steiner would have been content to adopt in the present spiritual climate—which, although they have several functions, have one that is peculiar to the Early Years of childhood. It is the function of 'shaping' matter.

We mostly recognize another person initially by their external appearance. The vast majority of us have ten toes and two eyelids as part of our universal human form, but even without going into DNA we can plainly see that each toe and each eyelid is unique. The attention Renaissance painters gave to the latter is there for all to behold on a thousand canvases. And with today's fashion of sporting nail varnish on toes as well as fingers, we have ample opportunity as we go about town to contemplate the former!

Educationally, the implication of these shaping, sculptural (etheric) forces was no trivial matter for Steiner. He regarded their function within the body as somewhat sacrosanct in the Early Years—something needing vital support from the adult world. Wholesome nutrition after breast-feeding, natural, appropriate and adequate clothing, an environment that recognizes the tender nature of the young child's sense organization, the build-up of hygienic habits, a fair degree of regularity during the course of the day, a peaceful 'rhythm' at bedtimes, space for creative play, opportunity for purposeful imitation . . . all have their part to play. But what should *not* encroach on the processes that are taking place in the organization of the etheric is *formal* education. Structure, yes. Demands on the memory, no. Spontaneously active participation, yes. Expectancy on behalf of adults of being able to regurgitate or retain what has been experienced, no.

As parents we are aware of children's physical development in several ways: growth, changes in digestion, cutting of teeth, muscular development to support crawling, standing and walking, and so on. Their etheric nature is tied up with all this, but as it takes place essentially out of sight our awareness tends not to stretch so far. Depleted life forces in the early years will have a lifelong effect.

The emphasis on the process and the importance Steiner attached to it culminates at around the seventh year. In referring to the seven-year cycle regarding the replacement of cells in the body (another function of our etheric organization), Steiner highlighted the significance of the eruption of the second teeth. The cells that form the milk teeth are too hard simply to be replaced, as is the case with other cells in the body. Hence, they are pushed out by the still stronger permanent teeth. This process, Steiner pointed out, is a telling sign for what is happening etherically in the child's nature. Not that one should only take cognizance of the change of teeth to ascertain whether a child is broadly speaking moving from one phase of development to the next. Other signs that the life forces have completed their approximately seven-year function need also to be taken into account.

In considering what happens to these forces during the succeeding phase of child development, Steiner harnessed the concept of *metamorphosis*. The life forces do not vanish or even simply transform their activity elsewhere, laterally, as it were. They go through a process of metamorphosis. This entails a 'move' from their scene of activity being in the *body* (sculpting matter) to being active in the *soul*. Memory now becomes accessible to the child *at will*, which invites and makes sense of formal education. The child's incessant outer activity takes a step inward though the brooding adolescent is still something beyond the horizon. And the faculty emerges in the mind which we have already referred to in an earlier chapter as *picture thinking*.

Two of the most common forms of 'damage' done to childhood in our times (the expression, damage, being first popularized some years ago by a Hungarian professor) are: (i) to 'educate' so that formal learning begins prematurely, i.e. before the life forces have completed their function here described; and (ii) once it *is* time for formal learning, to adopt educational methods that are in a form (usually rational) that ignores the child's faculty of primarily living in inner images.

Having dwelt on the early years vis-à-vis the life forces, let us therefore cross the watershed and look more deeply into the nature of picture thinking and its application in education.

Picture Thinking

'The pictures are so much better!'

The incident was related by A.C. Harwood to us students who were on the last teacher training seminar he was to direct (1963/4). It was a conversation he had with a small boy whose parents had just invested in a television. Harwood was curious to know the boy's reaction. 'I prefer radio,' he replied—'prefer' doesn't sound like the vocabulary of an 8-year-old but that was how Harwood reported it—'I prefer radio: the pictures are so much better!'

Many radio productions go out of their way with sound effects and other accompanying devices to help the listener visualize the situation, but to categorically state that the radio experience was a *pictorial* one went farther than Harwood had supposed possible. Even when you know 'theoretically' that humanity has gone through a stage of picture thinking and that, true to the principle of philogeny repeating itself at the ontogenetical level in the consciousness, *such* an affirmation can come as a shock to the mental system.

Steiner frequently exhorted the first group of class teachers at the Waldorf school to 'teach in pictures'. This would suggest three things. Firstly, that being highly educated (PhDs seemed to flock to the Waldorf standard, and that was long before our present generation where the degree is slowly beginning to have a ten-a-penny feel about it) they had schooled themselves in a certain type of thinking—conceptual rather than pictorial. And, despite there being ample opportunity for those PhDs through the prominently narrative nature of the Waldorf curriculum, living in pictures didn't come easy. Secondly—and this is conjecture on my part—although they *knew* its pedagogical importance and were intellectually convinced of its relevance for child development, *and* although they truly carried out the indication to the best of their ability in their praxis, in spite of all that, it had not yet penetrated the heart, not yet become married to belief, not yet become second nature, and certainly had not yet become part of what Steiner later somewhat paradoxically referred to as a consciously developed 'pedagogical instinct'. Thirdly—and this is only very seldom iterated, if at all—while the teacher may 'teach through pictures', simultaneously the children *learn* through pictures. The teaching is not merely a form of 'entertainment' that happens to be taking place in the classroom instead of at the theatre!

As this is so fundamental to an understanding of Steiner education, I would like to pursue the matter in some depth with the help of an extremely fascinating—and in my experience, unique and uniquely revealing—example.

In a Waldorf school situated in Hermanus (a resort on the famous 'garden route' of the Western Cape in South Africa) I witnessed the following. I was invited to a Class 1 main-lesson. The majority of the class came from Xhosa-speaking backgrounds. They had gained sufficient English for the language of the lesson to be conducted in English, the medium stipulated for education in today's rainbow-nationed South Africa. It was evident that their English served them adequately for all aspects of classroom management, instructions for movement, the saying of rhymes and verses, rhythmical counting, conversation with the teacher and the like. But when it came to story time, the school had appointed a native-speaking Xhosa woman to translate each sentence as the narrative unfolded.

I was seated at the side of the room from where I could see the children's facial expressions. No doubt their understanding of the English version varied according to each child's ability; and knowing that it would be translated, no doubt the teacher allowed herself to be freer as far as vocabulary, phrases and idioms were concerned than in other parts of the lesson. So no doubt the enhanced English that resulted meant that the Xhosa-speaking children's faces appeared more deadpan than at other times, and allowances should be made for that. But this does not detract from what I saw as a revelation. When the children heard the story retold in Xhosa, their *own* language, their facial expressions sprung to life, echoing every shade of feeling that the characters in the story were undergoing. The contrast was unforgettable. It was as if you were running a video but every few moments you constantly stopped it, resulting in: stillness, *animation*, stillness, *animation . . .*

The phenomenon clearly demonstrated how strongly one kind of language evoked the picture thinking in the children's souls, and how the other did not. Moreover, a further contrast was evident from the expression on the faces of the white English-speaking children in the class. One might have expected a kind of group psychological see-saw to be going on—animated English-speaking children's countenances . . . animated Xhosa-speaking children's countenances . . . and so on. But it wasn't like that. Firstly, the whites didn't reveal outwardly what was going on to the same extent as did the blacks—from which one should not deduce that it wasn't going on, or indeed that the image-making activity wasn't going on just as powerfully in the souls of the whites, for there was no doubt about their being inwardly equally entranced by the story. Secondly, the whites had the opportunity to linger with the image, since they were obviously, if subconsciously, aware that no new image was being presented by the Xhosa translator. Psychologically one might say that the plank of the see-saw was going up and down to its fullest extent on the Xhosa side of the fulcrum, whereas on the English side the rotational movement was less but that the enjoyment of the 'ride' was unhindered notwithstanding.

The rapt attention of both sides, however, left one in no doubt that profound educational experiences were taking place: the *picture of the story* spoke a language that was as 'loud and clear' to their child consciousness as a lucid piece of prose might be for a rationally orientated mind. Furthermore, just as the rational mind gains knowledge, information, wisdom from the *spoken word* (written too) so does the image-making mind gain equally (i.e. learns) from the *spoken picture*. In the former case, the knowledge resides somewhere at the level of crystal-clear consciousness; in the latter case, it resides in a more dreamlike state. The vital thing for the educator to know is that whatever the picture (in the story) contains as truth *is conveyed*. Through this medium, the children *are learning*.

If one looks at the whole journey from childhood to adulthood, it is self-evident that the *degree* to which children are able to imbibe knowledge and wisdom from pictures must change with their development. This must be catered for by the class teacher as he or she travels through the eight-year journey of the Lower School. During these years, as crystal-clear thought emerges from dreaminess in the child's consciousness, so the teacher's use of pictures must change.

In the history of civilization one observes that the Greeks were abundantly inspired by their age-old mythology while at the same time—and surely 'same' can apply to hundreds of years in terms of world history—they gave birth to that kind of thinking which we pursue today under the headings of numerous -ologies and -osophies. (One wonders if they had both hemispheres of the brain equally developed.) In the children's journey through the Lower School the last really full presentation of mythology that they experience is, coincidentally, at age 11 in Class 5, which happens to be Greek mythology. In the next school year, *without altogether abandoning pictures* of course, those aspects of *sharpened thinking* which are immanent begin to be cultivated through the study of deductive geometry and in other ways.

All this is not to say that the modern adult has no time for pictures. Those multi-millionaires in the movie, magazine and media industries would be in danger of becoming penniless if that were the case. But as far as child development is concerned, it is vital to 'get it right', to keep pace with the child's changing consciousness. In this respect the twofold pedagogical danger exists: at one end of the spectrum, to 'talk down' to the older child (use pictures in a way that the child has grown out of); at the other end of the spectrum, to present the content of the lesson in such dry, abstract or conceptual terms that the child cannot relate to it (boredom is possibly a symptom that this is happening).

If picture thinking arises once the child has crossed the threshold of consciousness at age 7, then the onset of rational thinking characterizes the next great watershed in child development. This takes place in that only too well-known yet grossly misunderstood phase we refer to as *adolescence*. The adolescent period is a moveable feast if ever there was one— indeed, so moveable that one sometimes wonders if half the adults on Broadway aren't still indulgently passing round the claret and tucking obscenely into the enticements of the dessert trolley. But let us not race ahead.

Behind the Scenes of Adolescence

'We're doing some smashing songs with Mr Masters!'
This was feedback I got from a parent of a 12-year-old. It was way back in the late 60s; it's not likely that today's youth would use the term 'smashing'! This was a time in my teaching career when I taught some class singing. The class in question was boy dominant, though numerically fairly well balanced. A particularly vibrant group, it had hockey players who got selected for their county and suchlike. I dug out a mixture mainly of colossal Schubert *Lieder* and Handel arias—nothing puny which they would inwardly be unable to respect. They learnt an impressive repertoire over a period of some three years (ages 11–14), which they sang somewhat like angels clumping around in Welsh rugby boots! Their class teacher had died unexpectedly when they were aged 11. Whenever they sang Gluck's 'Ché farò senza Euridice' in memory of their loss, it could bring tears to your eyes. But as good fortune would have it, they attracted a successor who was a godsend. This teacher took them through to Class 8, and helped them conquer all the adolescent peaks with flying colours.

That feedback somehow reassured me of something that I felt in my bones: you have to *stretch* adolescents—within reason, of course. Introduce them to and challenge them with the best and then accompany them with all your drive and enthusiasm while simultaneously being at your most proficient in classroom management.

In terms of age, adolescence is tricky to pinpoint. You think you're through the worst and then another glass-panelled door gets shattered. Still more thresholds to go! In terms of human development, however, the briefing is clear.

We are dealing with something that takes us *from childhood to youth* and, if at all possible, youth full spent so that a mature adult will emerge, bursting with Glad Day and the will to put teenage ideals into some sort of practice (however modified their final form may be).

So does this mean that adolescence doesn't fit neatly into Steiner's notion of life flowing in seven-year phases? Yes and no. The spectacle of the immature adult playing with technically mature weapons of mass destruction suggests that we pay dearly for rushing ourselves through childhood into youth with its exploration of the delectable forbidden. Such youth (misspent as it used to be called) seems to mortgage *maturity* in such a way that we sweat away for decades in our effort to acquire ownership.

That's the No, the unfinished business of adolescence. The Yes—it *does* fit into Steiner's concept of seven-year phases— can best be seen, perhaps, if we consider the analogy of birth. At birth, there's the severing or shrivelling of the umbilical cord. But there's also the antecedent and preceding phases. Gestation precedes birth, and a phase epitomized perhaps by the child at the mother's breast, of close dependence on the mother, follows. Thus if the midwife of physical birth is flanked by her two companions *conception/pregnancy* and *weaning*, we may look for their equivalent in the analogy of the 'birth' of adolescence. Steiner termed this *astral birth*. At age 7 we witness the liberation of the etheric forces, at age 14 the emancipation of the astral forces.

Plus or minus!

And there's the rub. The medical profession has got us accustomed to thinking in terms of normality/regularity as far as the *physical* body is concerned. The normal period for pregnancy, the use and abandonment of reflexes of the newborn, the focusing of the eyes, the cutting of the teeth ... right through to the loss of eye-muscle accommodation, menopause and the coming of old age. But even with physical development there is an 'acceptable' range for individual deviation. With a member of the human being that has a *meta-physical* dimension, the range is even wider. However, that doesn't mean that we are doing the child a service, as he or she is 'rising' from childhood to youth, if we simply shove him or her blindly onto the bandwagon of 'acceleration'. Particularly if we purport to be professional educators, it surely behoves us to be conscious of the gestation period of adolescence, of puberty itself (which might be considered the equivalent of the severing of the umbilical chord) and of the period following puberty when the slow weaning of the adolescent towards *self-responsibility* takes place.

Some of the most disturbing reading—yet at the same time enlightening—that has come my way over the last three decades has been *Evolution's End* by Joseph Chiltern Pearce (HarperCollins 1992), world-wide lecturer on human intelligence. The author cites numerous reports on research into 'brain growth spurts' which has been carried out principally in North America, and has been looking at how certain cells in the brain are annihilated during adolescence, i.e. those cells of the brain that have not been myelinated during childhood. Myelination consists of a protective layer that is resistant to the chemical 'clean up' going on at age 11+. Protection will have arisen through non-rational forms of thought in childhood. Examples come to mind principally from the arts and various forms of movement. Reading something like *The Lord of the Rings*, one imagines, might be another example. What I found disturbing was that not only did this affect the brain's potential to provide a *mirror for mental activity* such as imagination (the metaphor is mine and not the researchers') which we associate with the right hemisphere. It also strongly suggests that the function of the left hemisphere is impaired since the two hemispheres cross-fertilize.

That is: a 'healthy' right hemisphere potentially supports the left hemisphere with its rational, academic-like thinking mode. Thus, if we damage the right, the left will also be weakened—though here one is thinking of damage *by default*, the valuable cells not having been protected during the pre-adolescent years by an approach to education that takes seriously this aspect of child development into account.

So back to those 'smashing songs'.

At age 11+, the young human being, as far as neural development is concerned, has been through all its brain growth spurts and has the 'equipment' needed to develop what is needed in adult consciousness (left hemisphere emphasis). However, to *maintain* this neural equipment that the adolescent/adult will use for rational thinking, artistic activities, to put it broadly, will be—and will have been— necessary (right hemisphere emphasis).

Thus, the educational benefits of the arts, both performing and visual, in Waldorf education take on a new significance. On the one hand, they give a right hemisphere emphasis to brain development; on the other hand, they contribute towards protectively myelinating the layers of brain cells that otherwise get 'cleaned up'.

Steiner placed considerable emphasis on the *psychological* consequence of this. The physical maturity of the youth at puberty, combined with their mental awakening, means that their interest in the physical is doubly enhanced. This side of the child's nature is catered for in the rich and varied science curriculum that forms main-lesson material during the last seven years of the pupils' school career. An engaging interest in science helps direct outwards their awakening awareness of the physical plane of existence with its laws that are deemed to govern it, rather than the awareness becoming an unhealthy preoccupation with their own physical bodies. To this end, craft lessons take place in which the physical properties and potentialities of various media are explored, e.g. iron, silver, copper, willow, wood, fabric, stone for carving—all used in the making of well-designed but nevertheless utilitarian objects.

Equally important for the development of the whole child are the lessons in the arts. In the last three classes of the Lower School, these essentially continue the fundamental work in the arts of the first five years, but now with a significant change in direction in which the pupils are led to become familiar with what constitutes *style*. Particularly is this so in Class 8 in which the elements of poetry are studied in their stylistic dimension. Similarly with music. In connection with this age, Steiner spoke of comparing the styles of Brahms and Beethoven—an increasingly tall order in a world where this kind of music features less and less in most people's cultural experience. Be that as it may, rather than the school using that as an excuse for diluting Steiner's intentions, it can *provide* experience for the pupils that may be lacking from their daily lives: reading 'classical' literature, reciting in chorus some of the acclaimed highlights of poetry, singing some smashing songs(!) and, where at all possible musically, playing instrumental music both solo and in ensemble. It goes without saying that the first five classes will have laid down sufficient foundation skills to make all this possible.

Connecting even more closely with this artistic stream that flows through Waldorf education—a stream the prominence of which hardly needs emphasizing here, since it has attracted so much publicity over the years—are the *aesthetic main-lesson blocks* in the four Upper School years. Though not necessarily exclusively, each year concentrates on one of the arts, approaching it from the point of view of aesthetics: the visual arts (painting and sculpture) in Class 9, world literature in Class 10, music in Class 11, and architecture in Class 12. Thus, on the assumption that the pupils will have had/be having an ongoing experiential relationship with the arts in question, through the main-lesson block, an opportunity is provided for such experience to be 'raised' from the sphere of artistic *creation* to developing an *appreciation* of what can be observed and given considered thought.

All the foregoing provides rich cultural nourishment for the young people as they emancipate themselves from the ambience in which their childhood has been embedded, through the increasing experience of personality which is the result of the astral birth.

Our next step will be to look at some of the components that cause individual character to shine through the universal trends outlined here and in the preceding chapters, components that give distinctiveness to each child.

Individuality

'I can do I shoes up I-self!'

It was mid-afternoon. The just-about-to-be 3-year-old had had her after-lunch nap and was getting ready for her usual stroll in the park. She had never said 'I' until this moment, but had always referred to herself by the name that everyone called her—or occasionally 'me'. All in a flash that pre-'I' phase became past history. Just as Van Gogh would seem to have turned a corner when he produced his paintings and drawings of working men's shoes (1887/8)—and, goodness, how destiny-battered he ensured they looked—so this toddler turned a corner in her life's journey, also over a pair of shoes. (Well, if our feet didn't lead us to our destiny, where would we be?)

Although preceding chapters have already unpacked a lot of Steiner's notions of childhood, it might be useful here to put it in the following nutshell: *three seven-year phases which lead to the crowning moment of 21 when the ego reputedly comes, and in earlier traditions was acknowledged as coming, into its own.*

Ego! Unlike some of his contemporaries, Steiner used the term to signify that member of the human constitution which singles him/her out from the other kingdoms of nature. At the same time, Steiner was acutely aware that the ego (or 'self') carried various connotations and was experienced in different degrees. The connotations present the philosopher with a veritable labyrinth, which we shall attempt to skirt round, mindful of the confusion that could arise were we to stray into it too far, namely, the double, the alter ego, the entelechy, the 'all too human', egotism, Steiner's own concept of higher self and lower self, and so on. As to different degrees of experience, the child insisting on doing up her own shoes was clearly permeated with a strong sense of ego presence. At the same time, one can't but help think that she couldn't possibly have been consciously aware of that presence. It simply flashed out like the tongue of a chameleon, but nevertheless left its mark as if it had been three penetrating strokes on a kettledrum: *I . . . I . . . I . . .*

Different degrees of 'I'-awareness and 'I'-presence weave like warp and weft through human life. The growth and decline of the *physical* body spans a whole lifetime, traditionally three-score years and ten. And childhood sets us off on this journey with its three seven-year phases.

The rhythm of the *etheric* organization is more like a voyage than a journey. As a sequel to the seven years in harbour, the next septennial period takes place in calm waters in which the etheric nature of the child comes to the fore. There are the joys of swinging on the overhanging branch of a tree or a dangling rope, hopscotching along the slabs of an old stone pavement, hearing a favourite story, picnicking by a favourite water splash, setting off each season appropriately clad for blackberrying down the lanes, kite flying on the common, mushrooming in the woods, tobogganing down the slopes. Some of these may be difficult for parents to provide in an urban setting, but not entirely insuperable. Yet, where there's a will . . .

Adolescence—strongly connected with ages 14–21—is not content to safely hug the shores of the familiar and well beloved. Hoisting its ensign of exploration, the *astral* nature of the adolescent seeks its exit from childhood/youth into life. School lessons will thrive on *freshness of approach*. Each week needs to feel as if it's striding somewhere. Teaching material must offer grist to the mill of *awakening to the world*. Any teacher who is fortunate enough to have some free rein, of course, can work with these precepts. In Waldorf schools the underlying principles become a conscious and integral part of the pedagogy.

Finally the *ego*. Like the glint of mysterious red or some other unexpected colour that is discovered by tilting an opal in the light, the individual ego is always a force to be reckoned with. In the baby it is as if the ego lies beyond what we see gazing through those all-seeing eyes in the cradle. Like a cosmic sphere of thistle-down floating with its precious seed—minute by comparison yet carrying the germinal basis for a new life—the ego slowly descends towards incarnating into life and body.

Then the 'I shoes I-self' door bursts open. The *presence* of the 'I' is palpably stronger; but the *self-awareness* of that presence still has some time to wait. The fabric of ego-presence and ego-awareness one could say is a *unique and purely individual matter.*

We are back again at the concept of what distinguishes humanity from the other kingdoms of nature. No wonder Steiner advised the teachers to take a moment each day to create a 'quiet time' in which each pupil that one has taught passes momentarily but consciously before the mind's eye.

To take the metaphor one step further and give it a slight twist: we compared the development of the physical body with journeying to the harbour, the etheric development with a coastal cruise embarked upon at age 7, and we presented the astral nature as an ambitious expedition on the high seas heading towards hitherto unseen distant shores. Against this setting, the ego would therefore tally with the challenge of exploring the uncharted territory following landfall. The teacher's task is to keep track of the strength, beauty and moral integrity of the ego-presence/ego-awareness, and to assist whenever and howsoever might seem appropriate.

But precisely because of the presence of the ego, other

qualities that we associate with childhood and youth take on an individual colouring.

In particular, there is the *budding personality*, which reveals itself during adolescence, in which youth is constantly flexing the muscles of its opinion, frequently arguing that black is white, and the next minute vice versa, going through its emotional pendulum swings and so on. We are only too well aware of all the symptoms.

This is the age (14+) in which we see qualities such as burning enthusiasm, unflappability, clamour for attention, long-suffering, emerging balance, quiet revelation; these are spread like a vaulting constellation in the soul of each pupil, from where they become visible in various and fluctuating degrees of luminosity. The adolescent needs assistance in developing these qualities. Several Dutch anthroposophical doctors, out of their knowledge of the healing forces that work in medicine, have engaged over the years in modest research as to how these qualities relate to planetary influences. Teachers may be helped by resorting to such research, but whether they take that route or some other, it behoves them to engage with the adolescent on this level as one of their top priorities, albeit via the 'subject' (drama, chemistry, economics, and so on) for which they are timetabled.

Working backwards to the Lower School (ages 7–14) we come to the child's *temperament*. With its roots in Greece and the Middle Ages, a thoroughly modern, spiritually scientific understanding of the temperament and the part it has to play in human development was for Steiner a pedagogical lodestar. 'When you speak the child's name, express the temperament,' is advice that he gave. That would suggest that, just as the *curriculum has its core subjects* (the modern equivalent of the three Rs, and also in Waldorf the three 'arts' of colour, form and tone), so for these years, *taking the temperament constantly into account* is at the very kernel of Waldorf pedagogy.

Along with the physical body, each pupil in the class has been born with his or her temperament. But it somewhat bides its time before taking on, so to speak, the title role of personal development. For the teacher to *understand* how the four temperaments work—phlegma, choler, melancholy and sanguinity—Steiner advanced the approach of the Middle Ages (based on the 'humours') to more metaphysical considerations, such as the temperaments' propensity for *interest* in the lesson being taught. Is the interest easy for the teacher to *gain* (as is the case with the sanguine or choleric temperaments) or difficult (melancholic, phlegmatic)? Is the interest easy for the teacher to *retain* (as with the choleric and melancholic) or difficult (sanguine, phlegmatic)? From here it was a matter of retracing one's steps: Why is this so? And working forwards: What are the appropriate pedagogical measures and responses?

If the temperament is going to *serve* the adult, its positive aspects will need to be developed and harnessed. Lest the temperament *rule* the adult, its negative aspects will need eliminating. How to do all this in these formative years through form drawing, story-telling, movement, mathematics, seating order in the classroom, etc. became a fundamental part of the Waldorf teachers' training and, from that, something that Steiner ideally expected the Lower School teacher to develop as a kind of *professional second nature*. Though the class teacher, in particular, can't be expected to be an expert in all the subjects she has to teach (mythology, astronomy, mathematics, music, painting, physics, chemistry, biology, to mention a few), she can be expected to become a teacher who raises her vocation to high professional levels—much as the professional pianist raises her skills to levels to which the amateur can hardly aspire. 'Practice makes perfect' might apply in both cases, only with the pianist it is a matter of 'releasing' notes from the published manuscript into the realm of sound while the Waldorf teacher is teaching without notes, extempore, yet aiming to do so artistically with equivalent professional skills.

Still stopping short of going into fine curricular or methodological detail, the above aims to give an impression of what teachers in Waldorf schools take into account when educating. On the one hand, the comprehensive study of human development in childhood provides ongoing material for private and faculty-based research. On the other hand, the teachers' daily contemplation of all children in turn ensures that the unique gifts with which they are endowed as well as the drawbacks and obstacles with which they have to contend are perceived and understood educationally. Then it is a matter of professionally assisting in sending into the world human beings who have or will be able to develop the capacities to self-direct their lives in full accord with their own individual nature. Or, translated into the potent language of an about-to-be 3-year-old: 'I can direct I life I-self!'

The Threefold Organization of the School

'We're making Shabat bread.'

This was in response to my question: 'What are you doing?' It was a Kindergarten in Jerusalem, temporarily housed by the Municipality in the rambling basement of a fine old building in one of the 'neighbourhoods'. At one trestle table, plump little 4-year-old hands were grinding wheat. Other children were engaged in mixing dough. By the end of the morning the place was permeated with that unsurpassable smell that comes from bread baking as the dumpy little sun-round loaves—and a funfair of other curiously and creatively shaped pieces of dough that were set aside to be taken home—cooled on their racks during the story that preceded the Shabat celebration. Parents coming to collect their children tiptoed into the candlelight or waited reverently at the entrance porch. A final song, the Shabat candles extinguished, the good-byes exchanged, and the day was over. The room was given a final cleaning ready for the new week to start on Sunday, after which we all made tracks for the 'day of rest', the Sabbath.

A Waldorf Kindergarten in Jerusalem! Steiner envisaged many remarkable things, but one cannot help wondering whether he ever got quite as far as that! From virtually no Kindergarten movement in his day, this aspect of education has become one of the most important features of the contemporary Waldorf scene. In Lisbon, for example, although no school has as yet (2005) been established, the Steiner Kindergarten thrives and has extended its provision downwards to a Parent and Toddler group plus a room furnished with cots for the very young, still in nappies, whose parents both go out to work.

I shall go into this in more detail at a later point. Here I want to look at the organization of the faculty of a full Steiner school. It is only the middle of the three seven-year phases (7–14) that is fully represented in school. Though the Kindergarten may gradually become an option during babyhood, as with Lisbon, the child's first earth-welcome is in the home. At the other end of their school career, the students either step straight into life (which can be as early as 16) or into higher education. The first Waldorf school went up to Class 12. State examinations for higher education entry were taken at the end of a thirteenth class—referred to by Steiner as the 'exam preparation' class. He was adamant that 'achieving Waldorf' was the best preparation for the Abitur exam, though this did not rule out the acquisition of skills in the presentation of answers in the format required by the examiner.

But given these provisos, the organization of the school corresponds essentially with the three seven-year phases, mostly with separate faculty meetings for Kindergarten, Lower School and Upper School. The advantage of meeting separately in this way is largely a matter of time economy. At such meetings, practical arrangements are made by those, and *only* those, directly involved. And, more importantly from the inner aspect of the education, the meetings give an opportunity for those who arguably have the deepest understanding of the age group with which they are working to 'share their research'. From one point of view this is difficult to justify. In Steiner's day all heard what each had to say. With Steiner not being present, however, with his extraordinarily developed insights, there is something to be said for the one who is sharing her research getting feedback from those who know *first hand* what she is talking about. This said, as well as this 'division of labour', all schools have full faculty meetings so that there is ample room (a) for cross-fertilization between the three major sections of the school; and (b) for reports and information to be communicated. Without such faculty meetings, a school without a head teacher (which is how a Waldorf school operates) would be in danger of fragmenting, to say nothing of failing to achieve a unified ethos.

College meetings so-called are a separate issue and will be dealt with elsewhere. Here the opportunity will be taken to speak of the attitude towards her professional task and the relation towards the pupils in her care that distinguishes the teacher in each of the three sections of the school. This is related once more to the essential nature of the child. If the Kindergarten children express themselves primarily through *will*, pupils of the Lower School primarily through *feeling* and students in the Upper School primarily through *thinking*, how does the teacher adjust her pedagogy so that it supports a good relationship between herself and those she is educating?

The self-awareness which is increasingly permeating the consciousness of the Upper School students, together with the more focused awakening to the world into which they will soon be stepping, and for which they will become co-responsible, calls for drive, freshness, energetic thinking, enthusiasm, integrity, initiative, and unconditional honesty in the adult. This may be a tall order on a lugubrious Monday morning, or in the face of the kind of flak you might get if disciplinary action is called for. Nevertheless, it cannot be gainsaid. If the students don't find these qualities in their teachers to inspire them both in the subject matter as well as in their outlook on life, they will assuredly turn elsewhere for their self-chosen role models. This might be anything between the most estimable and the most despicable (the latter have easy access to young people's lives, appealing on the media, or through economic power influencing lifestyles at various levels via the market)—who is to say? Perhaps the

Upper School teacher's best coat of arms would be tripartite, a third depicting a *fellow researcher* who has strenuously trudged down long roads of enquiry before, another third a *brotherly/sisterly life-traveller* who has already become a bit travel-wise and, at the same time, the third third a person who, while sitting at the same round table as them, has been put in a position of *responsibility* for the overall conduct of the students, answerable to the school community as a whole, in so far as it is striving to become a harmonious community in which the self can also find free expression.

The key Steiner gave for the Lower School teacher's relationship with her pupils can be summed up in the word *authority*. In his view, pupils in this age group (7–14) require authority figures amongst their adults. Teachers will do well if they strive to become such figures. For the pupil of this age, a loving feeling for the authority of the teacher can arise, if it is embedded in *artistic* experience. The souls of the pupils are enriched through beauty. Day in, day out, they practise the arts, both performing and visual. Indeed, Steiner recommended that the very first Lower School lesson begin precisely in this vein.

Now the teacher has many artistic skills that must be 'performed' in the classroom. We have already seen that paramount is the *art of teaching* itself, but of course there are all the lesser arts to be continuously honed: the use of the voice in lively, image-filled storytelling, the use of the hand in writing gracefully on the chalkboard, the expression of beauty in the arrangement of the classroom and so on. This is not to mention the obvious: the ability to paint beautifully, draw elegantly, sing musically, play an instrument adeptly, move rhythmical exercises or country dances deftly, as well as 'perform' any other arts that may come her way. Small wonder that teachers find hours in the day in short supply! Steiner's point is that, buoyed up by such ever present artistic experiences, that element in the pupils' soul which thrives on authority will be able to extend admiration for the teachers' artistic skills into those other two spheres of discipline: the *behavioural* and the discipline of *learning* itself. That is, when the teacher needs to resort to what we think of as 'disciplinary action', providing she metes out discipline *fairly,* of course, the pupils readily accept her decision. Her word goes. Or when the teacher conducts the class through subjects that perhaps are tough going (mathematics for some children frequently crops up in this category), or less than favourites, the pupils are content to follow her up the steeper gradients that have to be climbed in acquiring knowledge.

In Kindergarten, the watchword usually cited is *imitation*. The adult does something; the children want to join in, impelled by their inherent imitative capacity. Drawing further on Steiner, we can go deeper into this, in that he recommended that as far as inner attitude is concerned those who have care of children aged 0–7 will do well if they cultivate a *priestly* mood.

This is easily open to misinterpretation. Anthroposophy is not a religion; and while generally helping priests who sought his professional advice, Steiner took special care to dissociate the work of the religious movement to which their work related from the anthroposophical movement. This was in marked contrast to the representation on the Anthroposophical Council that educationists, performing artists, mathematicians and astronomers, people at work in the humanities, doctors and others enjoyed.

So how do we understand this advice about priestliness? Going right back to Melchizedek, the priest who ministered to Abraham, we may take the priest's task as to invoke the spiritual via the ritualistic treatment of earthly substances so that it enters aspects of daily life. Examples are so plentiful amongst religious customs of all kinds as to be superfluous here. From this point of view, the Kindergarten teacher need search no further. Of course, the question of priestlike *rituals* does not arise in this respect. But whether she be shelling peas, setting tables, helping wash hands, cleaning windows, winding skeins of wool, she is engaged with one earthly substance or another. In whatever terms she thinks of it, her 'priestly' attitude will lead her to be aware that the earthly substance is part of creation (some would say God-given), and that in so far as human beings make use of it they have cause to be grateful. The result? The children, imbibing the teacher's *gratitude* for what is given and her reverence towards substance, are thus moved to imitate.

Thus any visitor to the Kindergarten will see the children *with their teacher* learning through doing: holding the skein of wool while the teacher winds it into a ball, breathing on the window pane to wipe away a smudge and make that last bit of glass sparkle, tidily putting back the towel onto its hook after washing their hands, placing mugs by each chair ready for snack time, determinedly slitting their little thumb nails into pea-pods, or, if the visitor is specially privileged, *kneading dough for the Shabat loaves.*

In looking at the changing teacher-pupil relationship in the three sections of a Waldorf school we started with the eldest and ended with the youngest. We shall now dwell longer with the youngest and consider more deeply the spiritual nature of the child—this extraordinary phase of life through which humanity passes, of being born and sojourning *some years* in the state that we call childhood.

EARLY YEARS

A Forgetting

'Tell me what it's like. I'm beginning to forget.'

I have heard more than one version of the following story (which does not stem from my personal experience), but the differences only refer to the setting—the message remains the same in all versions.

A mother and her small child of about 4 came to visit a newborn. They went up to the 'nursery' in the house where the family lived and after a peaceful time of 'baby worshipping', the 4-year-old looked up and asked, 'Can I be with the baby on my own?' The two mothers, somewhat overtaken by the totally unexpected request, exchanged glances. Surprise, nay, astonishment, a flicker of doubt, puzzlement and even amusement mingled with adoration for the child passed in quick succession through that exchange. Of course, it was the baby's mother's prerogative to say yes or no, but there was clearly mutual consent, and so the two adults quietly closed the nursery door and went downstairs.

With the intercom switched on, after some moments they heard the little visitor ask the newborn the above question. It is usually taken to mean: What is it like in the world from which you have 'descended'? On reflection, though, the 4-year-old could have been referring to the state of being in utero or simply of being a newborn and lying 'helpless' yet snug in a cradle. Leaving aside the question of *how* a 4-year-old and a newborn communicate, and why the adults were asked to leave, I am here opting for the usually accepted version of the story which leads to: What is it like in the spiritual world? And perhaps even more significantly, the 4-year-old's perspective: What is it like in the spiritual world, *which I hope will remind me of what was also my experience before conception?*

This question leads us into the whole concept of the human being's having a pre-conceptual as well as a post-mortal existence. Those who discount the latter are almost certainly likely to discount the former. But the point here is one that Steiner considered important, particularly for the educationist, a role in which parents share, though not strictly speaking on a professional level. The spiritual entity in a human being belongs to the *eternal* realm, and merely connects with the body (*incarnates*) for the brief span that we think of as earthly life. For the present consideration, this need not lead us into the question of repeated earth lives, either from an Eastern or Western viewpoint. We are focusing on human life at the outset, and the concept that a spirit being connects with the tiny newborn body with all its helplessness, vulnerability, dependence and immaturity. Not that we are promoting the well-worn notion of *tabula rasa*, childhood as a blank slate onto which the adult world inscribes all the accumulated wisdom of past ages. Rather are we attempting to project, albeit in somewhat amateurish and simplistic terms, what that pre-conceptual state must be like. 'Tell me what it's like,' as the 4-year-old put it. This leads us to superimpose both 'the incarnating into that tiny body' *and* 'the contrast of having been in a world of spirit'.

The newborn's connection with its earthly environment is on the one hand limited. It will be *very* limited if the parents take up the advice that I once heard a painter giving to a parent, to drape the newborn's cradle with silk of a colour which the mother considers is in accord with the mood of her baby. If this is done, it means that most of the outside world is cut off from the baby's sense experience. The eyes when open see gently coloured light filtering down through the silk, the baby's ears hear hushed sounds (that unique peace of a nursery), its sense of touch is entirely sensitized by the clothing in which the child is enwrapped—though this is superseded when it is time to breastfeed.

This thumbnail sketch of the newborn's sense experience is a simplification, in some cases a gross simplification, but it is something that at least to some degree is common to all. Equally common to all is that the spirit of the child has been surrounded before birth and conception with other spirits. Amongst these, in Steiner's view, are spirit beings who endow the human being who is on the way to incarnation with those qualities that will be a prerequisite for taking hold of life on the earthly plane. The Grimms' story 'Sleeping Beauty' depicts these as fairy godmothers who present gifts at the child's birth.

Often the mother will have an inkling of the nature of her child during pregnancy, which may well result in her knowing the name by which the child is to be known. The name may encapsulate not only the qualities with which the child is endowed spiritually but also something of the future track in life towards which he or she may eventually be drawn. We read in St Luke's Gospel that the old Jewish high priest Zaccharias became spiritually aware of the name of his son yet to be born; moreover that his insistence on the name caused some consternation amongst relatives and friends, steeped as they were in Jewish tradition. It is not *only* mothers who are open to knowledge that comes from beyond the realm of normal sense-perception—from the so-called supersensible.

Though we find the poets referring to this earlier state of existence—for example, Traherne's 'How like an angel came I down...', and Wordsworth's 'Our birth is but a sleep and a forgetting...'—we do not intend to follow this line of thought further here. We are not seeking to pile up evidence which would corroborate Steiner's view of the pre-natal life, equivalent, say, to the Egyptian *Book of the Dead*. Suffice it to say here that some acknowledgement of the child's greater being (its *individuality* which has its roots in the spirit, or however we wish to refer to that pre-natal state) is a healthy attitude for the teacher to cultivate.

Such an attitude is an integral part of the teacher's self-development. It can help us teachers make the extra effort needed to *serve* the child's needs, recognize our own inner *limitations*, modestly begin to overcome them, and to treat the child with due *respect*. Teachers will wish for the child a rich unfolding of the *talents* with which he/she has been blessed. They will work harder to extend their own *pedagogical skills*, and build the inner strength to cope with the often *demanding pressures* of the classroom, school organization, collegial cooperation and occasional conflict, parental demands, bureaucratic interference, staffroom moods and politics. And, who knows, we may get a little in touch intuitively with the latest developments in those regions that are deemed by some to link with those higher realms from which our children have descended years after we have! After all, if the 4-year-old felt that the newborn could communicate on that level, there must be a way.

The Senses

'Why does some mans has woolly chins?'

The 4/5-year-old was gazing out of the kitchen window, which looked onto the drive. Up on the road, parents were passing to and fro, taking children to school; some of them, realizing the importance of walking wherever possible, were on foot. Fascinated, the small boy had noticed a father with a beard. It doesn't take more than two or three seconds for someone to walk past an entrance which is little more than a few yards wide, just enough for a car to get in and out. In those few seconds, the father's beard—not necessarily the first the boy had ever seen—had prompted the thinking, which in turn had prompted the question.

There is no need for me to go into the type of beard; 'woolly chin' says it all. Reputedly the Eskimo has many different words for snow, according to its various conditions. How linguistically creative we would have to become if we didn't have a specific word for beard: a 'dashing, jet-black hairy lip frame', perhaps, for the Mephistopheles who leads Faust out of one torment into another; a 'swathe of grey down that merges into the mists swirling around the castle battlements', perhaps, for facial hair out of which the grim visage of Hamlet's father's ghost peers; a 'ruddy thatch of stubble', perhaps, for Thrym the Norse giant's beard. Rather rambling efforts, but it's difficult to achieve the 4-year-old's succinct linguistic creativity. Out of the mouths...

The main purpose here is to look at what prompted the child's descriptive gush. The immediacy of the remark rules out premeditation. The bull-in-a-china-shop grammar, rampaging uninhibitedly through the sentence, rules out the possibility of manicured thought habits. The 'thought-fullness' would therefore appear to be prompted by the *sense impression*. In that they weren't voiced, we do not know what other details of the passers-by the child took on board, but we might safely assume they were equally camera-shutter snappy.

Not that this implies the objectivity of a camera that records every frown, furrow and pimple on the family photograph. But consciousness, unlike the camera, is always filtering what is observed, selecting details to focus on. Young children especially soak in, via their sense impressions, as much as any camera—indeed far exceeding the camera's ability if we bear in mind that the child is 'observing' with multiple senses, whereas the camera is confined to the visual. But where the camera is technologically icily accurate, the child's accuracy is empathetically wholehearted. The child's observation is or comes close to being self*less*; the camera's accurate record of what the lens 'sees' is self-*absent*. Thus we have objectivity in two polar opposite states of consciousness: the child with its lingering participative consciousness, drinking in what the environment has to offer, with all its senses and—as in this case—prompting mental activity; the camera (or tape recorder) fixing the 'living' moment onto film (or CD). The child is seeing, hearing, tasting; the camera etc. is mechanically reacting according to its technical construction.

Steiner likened the sensory nature of children to sponges. A sponge is non-selective. Ink, brine, cognac—you name it and the sponge will soak it up. We have seen elsewhere that the individuality of the young child may be strong—we meet an ego-presence even in the 'starry' eyes of the newborn—but that does not at the same time imply self-*awareness*. Sense impressions funnel liberally into the child's mental awareness, unimpeded by a high degree of self-awareness. The proverbial absent-minded professor is at the opposite pole.

'People passing by? Er, yes, I *think* so.' 'Chins?' 'Well, of course, they *must* have had.' 'Woolly chins?' 'Pardon . . .'

Some of those human faculties which Howard Gardener alerted the educational, psychological and medical worlds to through his research (1984, *Frames of Mind*) include 'intelligences' which Steiner, at the beginning of the last century, had firmly designated as senses. He enumerated twelve— innovative for an audience that had been brought up on the popular notion of five. These he divided into three groups of four, and linked each group in broad terms with *body, soul and spirit*—a familiar keystone in his world view.

The four 'bodily' senses are *touch, movement, balance* and a sense of *well-being*, the last being the most inward of the four. These are frequently referred to as the 'lower' senses. It is vital that the child's early life affords ample opportunity for the exercise and development of these four senses, be it in the home, the Parent and Toddler Group or in the Kindergarten.

The 'middle' senses are more familiar to us: *warmth, colour (sight), smell and taste*. These senses lead us more deeply by degrees into the *outer* object. The sense of sight (which distinguishes shape and form through colour differentiations) gets no further than the very surface of things. We scent something when its substance is perceived by our olfactory sense; through it we gain impressions that enter more deeply into the nature of the object. How cheated we feel if a red rose is scentless; how some people's appetites are quickened by the smell of fried bacon wafting from a neighbouring campsite; how obnoxiously we react—despite any sincere sympathies we may have—when someone is seasick! With taste we enter 'behind' the surface of things by dissolving the very substance itself on the tongue with the glandular excretion that is exuded through the gums. Think of the contrasting sensations of someone who wolfs down their fish and chips and the professional wine taster.

The 'higher' senses take us as far into the external world as sense-perception can go. They are *hearing* and what Steiner referred to as the sense of the *word*, of *thought* and the sense for the *other person's ego*. Less and less *outwardly* perceptible, these higher senses give us the possibility of entering 'sensitively' into the other one. With hearing we are still in realms that are not confined to the human. A braying donkey, a babbling brook, a plonking coconut, the clank of an old tram, the twang of a guitar, the crack of a hard-boiled egg, the wet slop of falling cow dung, the first few chirrups of the dawn chorus, the scrunch of tide-washed shingle all take us into worlds to which, without hearing, we would have no access. Through the sense of the word which quickens our inner perception a considerable degree more than does hearing, we enter into the other person's thought world. 'I hear what you say,' we comment when we have really gleaned the thought of the other one—all of which either cannot or has not been fully experienced through the actual words themselves. Finally the ego, which is the most veiled of all, frequently has little or no outer expression. Vocabulary is rich in words to describe what we see: obtuse-angled, bottle-green, russet, magenta, precipitous, obese, mottled, star-radiant, shipshape, scabby, concave, tied in a bow, and so on. For ego perceptions, by contrast, we may find ourselves searching: noble, a 'cowboy', butter wouldn't melt, dour, scrounger, an angel, upright, canny, warm. At the same time, it is clear that such expressions are not strictly confined to ego qualities.

The education of the senses continues throughout childhood. Richer will be the school experience of those who have been taught by people who realize the benefit of appealing to, and bringing into play, all twelve senses—in an appropriate way, it goes without saying. Pupils may well recoil or at least suffer if the educational diet relies almost exclusively on the sense of thought, and that relentlessly dry and intellectual.

Finally, it is worth pointing out that there is a slight emphasis in Waldorf Early Years education on the lower (bodily) senses, in the Lower School an emphasis on cultivating the four middle senses, and in the Upper School a presentation of material that particularly takes into consideration the need to stimulate the higher senses, these being particularly relevant to the young person's increasing awakening of an independent and original thought life.

We should guard against being dogmatic, however. The sense of thought of a 4-year-old on seeing a woolly chin may clearly be quickened. Or might it be even higher: the sense of ego?

Imitation

'This is a lorry; this is not a table, no.'

A child of about 5 years of age had been watching a coal delivery some days before. At least once a day thereafter the whole thing had been re-enacted with astonishing determination, as if the memory of the event lived in a realm inaccessible to adults or, at any rate, of little interest or value to them. Indeed, with some things one could go further. Jobs about the house or garden are for some of us chores that are one of the necessary labels attached to the 'cost of living'. If we caught ourselves, say, filling the dishwasher, putting correspondence into the filing cabinet or putting the petrol we use into the tank with anything approaching the gusto with which those same deeds can be seen imitated by small children, we would feel odd to say the least. Or another scenario: supermarkets would have to be drastically redesigned if space were allotted for a couple of hundred customers with their trolleys, strutting enthusiastically between gangways from one shelf to the next—instead of the way so many appear to be drifting along half in a dream!

The coal delivery re-enacted took place in various parts of the house. The 5-year-old child had reached that stage of play which tends to start with a memory; the memory becomes an urge; the urge prompts the fantasy; the fantasy looks around to see what objects can be roped into service to provide sufficient outer semblance for the imitative forces to pour themselves into *will*. (Though it smacks of it, this is not a deliberate parody of 'This is the House that Jack Built'!) When the child starts stumping around with cushion after cushion on his back and shoulders, imagining himself to be the coalman and the cushions to be coal bags, and hurling the imagined contents into an imagined coal bunker etc., we smile affectionately and call it *play*. The affectionate smile may be modified if the 'game' of coal delivery becomes elaborated to the extent that so much of the furniture in the house is commandeered as to jeopardize the functionality of the place. But that's us, *enchanted into the strong utilitarian dictates of life's chores*. The child's fantasy, on the other hand (putting memory into imitative action where *the object is enchanted into the mind*), works the other way. Likewise the cushion is liberated from its confinement to cushionhood into that world in which a cushion can quite happily become a coal sack, with a toasting fork becoming the delivery man's gear lever in the cab of the lorry, the kitchen table the coal lorry, and the human larynx (or rather, its virtuosic misuse) the sound of starting up an engine, of gear changing, and of the screeching of brakes at a traffic light or at the entrance of the next customer's driveway.

So many of the tributaries that descend into the valley of childhood flow together in play: the tributary of *fantasy*; the energetic expression of the child through *will*; the absorption of the world through the *senses*; the possibility of *gesture* alone being sufficiently suggestive 'language' to represent a world of outer objects; the hunger for and satisfaction derived from unadorned *repetition*; the unconditional trust that is expressed in the world as intrinsically *worthy* and hence the *devotion to the physical*.

One of the most pathetic stories ever related to me was of a lonely child who was admitted to a Kindergarten near Tel Aviv. Wan and timid, she remained on the periphery of the social scene, though happy to be drawn into what the 'teacher' was busying herself with. After some days, the child became accustomed to the ambience of the place. With her new found confidence she looked up at the teacher and pleaded, 'Please Tamar, will you *teach me how to play?*'

The pathos, of course, lies in the 'teach me'. A socially healthy child needs no more teaching how to play than a newborn healthy body needs teaching how to wet its diaper. This is not the place to investigate which of the tributaries had dried up in this particular case, but it would seem deep seated. Clearly the urge to play was there, otherwise the question would not have come with the wish to join in. Thus the problem would seem to have been in the region of the fantasy. If the mind can't yank the table from its table-ness into becoming the chassis of a coal lorry, then outer and inner worlds lack the potential of mutual oxygenation. But though the outer world is segregated into its multitudinous, dead, coal bag and cushion compartments of 'reality', make no mistake, the death blow has been dealt by the fantasy-bereft mind.

Waldorf Kindergarten teachers refer not merely to play but to *creative play*. Apart from the creativity abundantly manifest in play in these early years, the term would suggest that the source of the ceaselessly babbling tributary of fantasy is connected with creative forces. Not difficult to come to terms with if one considers the creative power of all that the child is experiencing bodily in its rate of growth (still phenomenal even though it has slowed down somewhat since being in embryo).

Thus, the child's abundance of creative forces, together with will-power virtually unimpeded by mundane logic, flow together in imitation. In the dreamy remark, 'The wind is blowing because goaty will need his scarf,' we have an example of play arising from some other source. Either the child's impulse to wrap a scarf round her cuddly toy goat's neck required that she (like Prospero who raised the tempest in Shakespeare's last play) considered it part and parcel of life to command the wind or she simply had not worked out the logic of cause and effect.

Here we need to follow the tributary of the child's inherent spirituality. We have already touched on this. The human spirit's journey towards incarnating takes place through a purely spiritual environment. From it, the dowry for the forthcoming life is received, received with unconditional trust, the trust that one will be born with the potential needed to fulfil one's life's task—whether that be poultry farming, turbine maintenance, fashion designing, tax collection or plain, humdrum robber-chasing (the task that fell to the Bremen Town Musicians!).

The momentum thus set up continues. Deep into the child's psyche is a voice which chants: *All that comes towards you is worthy of imitation.* Even with the child whose fantasy had been frozen (if that's a fair analysis), and who besought her Kindergarten teacher to teach her how to play, this impelling voice could not be silenced, though it took some time to become audible.

The implications for the adult and his self-development, of course, are also momentous. Can we live up to *being worthy* of being imitated? Mercifully, for many children, the moment of disillusionment in the adult world is kept somehow at bay. The momentum carrying belief into worthiness blinds the child to the inevitable cracks and blemishes in the fabric of our lives which we can't wallpaper over. Perhaps it is similar to the belief that the child has, say, in Santa Claus. The spiritual archetype is so strong that it eclipses the false beard or transforms the familiar voice of Uncle Willem into something that sounds from across the threshold—the threshold that divides physical and metaphysical or the real from the imagined, or, for the young child, that divides all the resonance, still echoing on from the pre-conceptual life, from the here and now—the clattery swoosh of helicopters and the anguished tally-ho of ambulance sirens, etc.

Finally a word of warning. The tributaries in the valley of

childhood flow from *both* sides of that valley. In particular, in the child's fantasy both from the imitative that is a continuation of the spirituality in the child's *pre-earthly* existence and from impulses that are *future-orientated* they exist side by side. Whilst the richness of the *past* lives in the child's whole makeup at birth, it is the *future* that lies dormant somewhere in the realm of intention, aims, aspirations. Nonagenarian reflection lies a huge way away.

The following incident shows how the adult needs to be alert to both tributaries at play. A couple who were attending a workshop I gave on child development explained that they were very new to Steiner's ideas. (The mother eventually became a Waldorf class teacher; the father pursued his academic career into the direction of higher education.) They had followed up the idea that the child thrives on imitation and introduced much into their home life that encouraged it, where before it had been absent—at least absent from their consciousness. They were also interested, however, in bringing some of the Waldorf Kindergarten ideas into the home, one of which had been watercolour painting. One of their children had delighted in the liquid colour provided to the extent of pouring out from the jar a stream of colour which flooded both her sheet of paper and an exciting acreage of the kitchen table. In pointing this out, and describing his mild shock at the bold transformatory effect that this had on the rest of the painting(!), the father in all seriousness commented: 'She had never seen me or her mother do this.'

He went on to ask me what I would have done in similar circumstances. Hesitating to jolt him further by saying, 'Probably joined in,' I simply volleyed the shot with, 'What *did* you do?' The participants of the workshop visibly effervesced at the reply: 'I allowed her mother to deal with it!' Looking at the subsequent careers of the parents 15 years later, the incident would appear to have been a stroke of fate for both.

With the early years, you never know whether the kitchen table is going to be a colour-flooded lagoon after it has served its purpose of being a coal lorry.

Will

'When that Mummy wash that Mummy's feet?'
It has become a well-established tradition that a repro-
duction of Raphael's *Sistine Madonna* be hung in a Steiner
Kindergarten. The above remark was made by a child who
had been contemplating it. I cannot imagine that the adult
standing by and overhearing the child (who was merely
'thinking' uninhibitedly aloud, of course, as is the case with
most children in such situations or when they are making the
sort of comments in stage whisper voices that make the
embarrassed parent wish the floor would open and swallow
her up!) would claim that the remark contained the kind of
out-of-the-mouth-of-babes wisdom that shed light on the
religious mystery contained in Raphael's masterpiece. So
where did the child's rhetorical question come from?
Questions are linked with perceptions. You would be
surprised if a blind person asked about the significance of a
particular shade of red used by a Renaissance painter, say, for
the robe worn by Mary Magdalene anguishing at the foot of
the cross. Yet perceptions are more than the mere registering
of percepts. We use the term 'percept' to designate the pure
impression an object makes. The drawings by Leonardo de
Vinci of the eddying, wavelike forms made by flowing water
indicate exceptionally acute perception—that is, the registering of what the eye can see. The 13 figures in the same
painter's fresco *The Last Supper* would indicate that his
powers of perception penetrated deeply into human nature as
well as being able to 'capture' outer form.
How many of us who try to cultivate deeply perceptive
observation have looked at the *Sistine Madonna* and even
noticed the feet all that much, let alone linked their

appearance with the fact that when you wash feet they first need to be bare? (Did it even get as far as a *train of thought* with the child?) A comedian might pick on such a detail in order to raise an irreverent laugh! But to be so vociferously in earnest as was the child...? The only point you have to make...? No hint of interpretation? No reference to the position of the child in relation to the mother? No acknowledgement that instead of sky above the clouds, where you might expect it, a clustered host of cherubic faces? Only... 'Don't just stand there: the bath water's getting cold!' (Now here am I, inadvertently erring towards comedy.)

To move from 'percept' to 'perception' in the above sense, the perceiver brings his or her inner life into play. The art critic brings a wealth of *knowledge* to focus on interpreting, explaining, commenting on what she sees. The churchgoer, on the other hand, brings the *feelings* he associates with the subject to bear on the picture. (Christmas cards often display pictures that many artists would rate as showing minimal artistic talent, while to the recipient whose Christmas is essentially a religious festival it is sufficient that the image reminds him of the Magi journeying from the East.) The art critic's perceptions may be principally guided by the intellect; the churchgoer's clearly well from the heart. But the child, bent on pointing the Madonna in the direction of improved hygiene, is coming from neither of these directions. In his case, it is a matter of sheer practicality, bodily function, daily routine, getting down to brass tacks—*will: Do something.*

This is virtually the antithesis of the child who, untrue to character, cannot summon up his will forces. How forlorn his voice sounds when he sidles up to you and sighs, 'I don't know what to do.' Yet even that gives us some small glimpse of his relationship to his will, in that as likely as not the momentarily will-bereft child is not looking for anything that will produce a *result*. He just wants to be doing. Even if the activity proves productive, he might later describe it not as, 'We baked biscuits,' but as, 'We did baking.'

While the artist uses *will forces* to paint, to draw, to dance, to act, they are, at the most, secondary to her art. The sometimes ivory-towered intellect goes even further: it can function devoid of outer action. This was Hamlet's enduring dilemma: his *mental activity* impeded rather than prompted his will to revenge his royal father's murder. 'Will' is at the other pole. It can be impervious to inner feelings or intellectual refinements. Doolittle, the dustman in Shaw's *Pygmalion* 'discovered' his fatherly feelings when there was suddenly money to be made out of his blood relationship to Eliza.

In the case cited of the child taking in the percept of the *Sistine Madonna* and responding out of pure will, it is not that the child had no religious feeling or was not attracted by beauty. It was simply that the dominance of will over thought and feeling in the child's soul coloured his perception. Attempting to encapsulate the psychological situation in words, it might sound something like: 'There must be something that the people in that picture could be—ought to be—*doing*. As for aesthetics and understanding, there's plenty of time for all that. Now it's sleeves rolled up.'

Blessed—certainly privileged these days—is the parent who has time (and patience) for his 3-year-old to 'help' when he's grating carrots, topping and tailing gooseberries, tidying a cupboard drawer, thinning out the Swiss chard, mending a fuse. Where it's purely imitation at play, the 3-year-old impinges less on daily life. There can be a whole wedding service being solemnized in the sitting-room, or the kitchen table can be converted into a fire engine tearing down the High Street through jammed oncoming traffic, or the umpteenth visit to Teddy in hospital (in the same ward as Granny) might be taking place in a corner of the bedroom, while you, the parent, are grating carrots, chopping chard, crushing garlic, frying onions, and blissfully preparing the evening meal, all in a lightning 90 minutes. But once you've attracted your toddler's 'help' (resonated the will through your own busyness), be resigned to dinner being delayed, with a potentially crusty wife and an impatient teenager on your tracks, and with all your kitchen tidiness temporarily hurricaned out of the window.

But also be resigned, or rather assured, that where you *can* accommodate your 3-year-old's giving vent to his will, bliss of a different order will follow, whose life-long benefits will far outweigh the ephemeral friction caused one evening by dinner being five minutes overdue.

This is not to suggest that modern life supports such an approach to child raising. Happy is he whose neck is not dangling in the noose of the mortgage gibbet, and who therefore has time to cook his child's meal without resorting to the freezered package and the microwave. And happy is the *will* of the child who has room to thrive in such a throttle-free home.

During an afternoon free from from lecturing, I was once visiting the Hermitage in St Petersburg. The crowd admiring Leonardo da Vinci's *Madonna and Child*—one of his rare completed works—fluctuated in size according to when the next coach party swept through the museum. On the occasion in question a woman in advance of her party thrust her way to the front, stood slightly at the side of the picture, glanced first through and then hastily over the top of her spectacles at the priceless masterpiece for two or three seconds, and with protruding neck exclaimed in a far from hushed voice, 'Well I'm damned!' before scurrying off to the next exhibit. It seems something of a bizarre contrast to the scene depicted at the beginning of this chapter, but one can often learn through shock. One was left with the feeling *'When that tourist wash that tourist's spectacles?'* or, translated for the non–6-year-old readers: When will she develop the perceptions that would enrich her life beyond all recognition?

Goodness

'Next time I'm going to have Mrs X!'

Most families, where there are young children, get used to their younger members coming out with radical statements, quaint and original uses of grammar, impossibly unanswerable questions, embarrassingly personal observations, undiplomatic declarations of truth and the like. If parents think they can keep a skeleton in the cupboard with a 3/6-year-old around, they are more than likely to have another think coming to them very soon.

Quite frequently, and amongst the most memorable of such remarks, these refer to non-visible worlds. With no preamble whatsoever, 'I wouldn't mind being God,' said a youngster who was gazing dreamily out of the bedroom window at a glorious winter sunrise—with the mother hardly able to breathe in her astonishment at the main clause and her totally vacant yet simultaneously mind-swirling anticipation of what might be coming next—'if it was my job to paint the sky,' he concluded.

Or another example, quite common compared with the uniqueness of the previous one, though the sequel would take some beating: having been asked *what God was like* as he was saying goodnight to his stepdaughter, the somewhat nonplussed questionee stammered something like, 'Well, you have to be very wise to know that.' The tiny bundle, tucked cosily into bed hardly needed to ponder before she countered, seemingly totally dispassionately: 'Well, I'll ask you again in a few year's time.' I've heard said that the stepfather gave up a lucrative career in accountancy and took up gardening!

But to return to Mrs X. The family in question were very

guarded when talking in front of the children, to the extent that when the youngest member—a good 70 years away from the threshold of death, if one goes by average life expectancy!—started speaking about the *after-life*, they were taken by surprise. They were even more surprised when she pressed the matter further with: 'When you're born again do you always have to have the same Mummy?' Here again, the person questioned had to take a fairly blind swipe at it: 'Oh no, of course not!' It was at that point that the remarkable choice was voiced, quoted at the beginning of the chapter.

Mrs X was a good friend of the family whom the child saw occasionally. She was not a close neighbour, however. With composed equanimity—perhaps in some of the more exasperating moments of family life, it might have been with amused relief!—the mother later wondered what it could possibly be about Mrs X that had caused her lively daughter to bestow such a double-edged-sword accolade upon her. But as the penning of the next chapter of that unusual piece of biography is by definition at least a lifetime away, we will have to give up the pursuit of the story.

But let us not leave the question of what gives rise to such a perception in a young child. What had she *seen* in Mrs X?

Even at a young age, it was plain to see that the child was sanguine—not pathologically so by any means, but fairly pronounced all the same. She therefore essentially took to what life brought, without much reserve. This meant that, viewed *outwardly*, she would have had good cause for singling out this or that friend from amongst the family acquaintances as a suitable future mother. Maybe she would have taken that in her sanguine stride anyhow, but the point here is to look more deeply into the matter.

Steiner held that it was *what you are* that mattered in your relationship to the young child. I take this to mean that what you think and feel *penetrates your whole being*. If this is, and has been, your normal disposition then you are a 'natural'. But it can equally well be a state that you strive to cultivate.

In the Lower School, 'what you are' is obviously not unimportant. The 7/14-year-old, however, is looking for those whose artistic 'touch' (in movement, speech, thought-processes, and even as it expresses itself in the everyday outer arrangements of life) is inspiring. By comparison, the young child thrives when its *bodily well-being*—which is not to deny psychological health—is in good trim. The Lower School pupil feels best when his or her *soul* thrives in the artistic ambience that the adult radiates. Perhaps one could say that, like the painter's canvas thrilling to the master touch of a paintbrush, the soul is nourished through beauty of all kinds.

If the *whole being of the adult* is permeated by positive, moral qualities, Early Years children, through their exceptional sensitivity, are drawn to this. Such a disposition of soul is an echo of the spiritual we touched upon earlier by which the self is impregnated and with which it is surrounded, so to speak, before birth and conception.

Much popular study has been focused in recent years on body language. During the political campaign to get recognition for Steiner education in the UK in the early 90s, the spokesperson for education of the party then in government very naively tried to win my vote by referring to the Opposition and saying, 'Don't be taken in by their smile, look at their teeth!' A will impulse which is truly rooted in the spirit will first permeate the soul and then become self-evident in body language, which a person either uses consciously or reveals unconsciously. Young children, with their multi-planar sensitivity, are usually highly 'literate' when it comes to reading this kind of language. Hence the importance of *gesture*.

In the very gesture by which the adult communicates, the child feels: you are joyfully welcomed; desist; come along and join in; blessings go with you on your way; take more care over how you sweep; are you listening to the story? that's lovely; yes continue; be patient for a moment; what a beautiful bunch of flowers; it's your *right* hand I want to shake; have you closed the door properly? that's enough now; time for grace; let's all sing together; aren't you glad you're snugly dressed on this frosty winter morning? here's a place for you beside me; it was really lovely to visit you. The gesture might be in the hand, arm or finger, the eye, the inclination of the head, or the facial expression. But it is gesture which has its origin in the spirit and then permeates the soul. And streaming through it is the *goodness* that emanates from the adult's whole attitude towards the child's well-being.

Goodness in this context is conveyed essentially in a non-verbal manner, which is not to say, of course, that the Waldorf Kindergarten is a silent place. That would be absurd. But the quiet buzz of voices, children and teacher is only what has risen to the surface of the *activity* going on. The teacher's actions, however simple the task, exude good will towards the child. The children's actions reveal how deeply contented they are to be in the presence of such an adult. This is irrespective of whether what they are engaged in flows from their impulse to reflect or imitate what they have taken in from the world around or whether their actions well up from the creative forces that flow as much *from* the future as *towards* it.

Education at the level of *will*, learning through *imitation,* perceiving and understanding through *gesture,* activity devoted to the *task in hand*, and from the adult, parent or teacher a quiet radiance of being which carries, perhaps, the riddle or even intuitive reminiscences of the spiritual endowment that the child received before birth—these are the waves that wash continuously on the shores of healthy Early Years education.

In such an atmosphere there will be nothing said, however frequently reiterated, that sounds remotely like platitudes. Every fibre of 'what you are' speaks. One 'Hello' streaming from the innate goodness of 'what you are' is worth more than a dozen new laws on social integration. One 'Thank you' welling from your grateful heart is worth more than a dozen sermons on acknowledging the input of others. The credentials of the teacher or other carer all hinge on whether his or her whole nature exudes *integrity of being*. If it does, just as the body will thrive from breathing fresh, unpolluted air, so will the soul-spirit nature of the child thrive from breathing an atmosphere in which goodness prevails.

Thank you Mrs X, we've got the message!

Movement

'Can we go again to the big sandpit?'

One of the treasured memories of many Israelis I have met is of visits they have paid to the Ramon Crater. This vast geological feature lies to the south of Beersheba, towards the Sinai on the Egyptian border. It is one of Israel's desert regions, loved for various reasons: it is far from the madding crowd; its humidity-free air is crisp and awakening; it evokes the feeling of utterly raw nature; its pristine cleanliness is stimulating; its teethlike geological formations around the crater's rim engender awe; the splendour and patchwork variety of its floor (slabs, pebbles, boulders, crystals, gravel, etc.) is a delight; it is a mineralogical treasure-trove; the rare carpet of delicate colour that springs up within hours if there is a springtime downpour is a wonder; and there is the splendour of its star-studded canopy each night.

All of this, however, completely escaped the urban-dwelling 6-year-old, at least in the immediacy of his young mind. What was memorable for him was his discovery of a new world—instead of a rather grubby sandy patch of four square metres outside the Kindergarten, here was a 'sandpit' that just went on for ever. His parents admired the subtle colours, the shapes and formations of the stones lying on the surface, photographed the jutting teeth of the perimeter towering up from where they stood at the base, stretched out on the sand and deeply breathed in the crisp, sun-filled air. Relaxed and thankful to be away from the nervous atmosphere of Tel Aviv, they sat and chatted by the camp fire in the stillness of the night. They were inwardly strengthened by the stillness and utter quiet all around. But what is all that to the limbs of a 6-year-old? For their son, it was a place to revel in because he could dig, make trenches, build mounds and dikes, walls and towers, form enclosures by sticking flat stones end to end in the gritty sand, pile up bigger stones into heaps, make viaducts, bridges, steps, monoliths and sand-castles to his heart's content. In a word, he could be engaged in timeless movement—albeit till the sudden flop came at the end of the day, and drooping lids led into sleep.

During the Early Years with which we are at present chiefly concerned, *will* expresses itself through movement. In later years, through having to concentrate on filling in a complex tax form, perhaps, we experience that *will* needs to be harnessed in our mental life. But for the young child, his seemingly never-ending activity in the limbs provides the outlet for *will*.

The Coldstream Guards sergeant barks his drilling orders: 'First man to . . . *move*.' There need be no immediate sense in the drill; just subject the will to the voice of command *without any intervening thought*, which might save life—or inflict death—in battle. The voice that the small child obeys is silent but equally impelling—it is the voice that stirs the limbs into movement.

Think of the healthy movable toys that children enjoyed in former rural communities: the hoop that the naked American Indian children on the high plateaux of the Andes whack with a stick and go gleefully bounding after as it rolls on its way; the Russian dollies that pull apart round the 'waist' and fit neatly inside one another; the Polish chickens whose pecking heads are merry-go-rounding whenever you twirl with your wrist the wooden ball that dangles from a hole in the middle of the board where they are pegged; or the Portuguese cyclist whose legs go busily up and down as, with a long handle, you push the contraption on which he is seated along the cobbled ground.

Steiner applauded *moving picture books* for this age, books that have cardboard tags sticking out from the pictures, which, when activated, cause some detail in the picture to move. Or they may have strings hanging from the bottom of the page: pull this one and the mother's arm sews a garment; pull that one and the horse nods his noble head and neck; pull this one and the girl waves goodbye to her parents as she sets off on her journey through the woods; pull that one and a dove flies out of the green foliage at the top of a great oak tree, and so on. Sadly such books can be rare commodities even in Waldorf Kindergartens; the market has a difficulty making them financially profitable.

Movement is educationally valuable on several levels. We have already seen that Steiner placed it among the twelve senses. This can be further explained. It is not the outer movement that is meant, though it goes without saying that outer movement has its purpose and can be health-giving. As one of the lower, so-called bodily senses, movement is a sense activity by virtue of the fact that we *inwardly* perceive where our limbs are (the foot and ankle and shin and kneecap and thigh and leg all move in harmony as we march up a flight of steps). The fingernail that scratches an itch at the back of the head does not need to fumble about to discover where the itch is. The hand that accidentally touches the hot stove instantly moves *away* from the source of discomfort and not along its surface. When we bend down to pick up a bucket by the handle we hardly give it a thought, unlike someone who may be learning Japanese etiquette and bowing to a mandarin or some other dignitary for the first time! We achieve success in these cases because we perceive our bodies with our *sense of movement*.

The second of these two levels is connected according to Steiner with the sense of word. We get a glimpse of this when someone is stuck for a word. There will often be a hand movement as if searching for the word—a flick of the fingers, a poised palm, tapping the temple with the fingertip ... a variety of gestures.

The child's *dialogue* with its environment, however, is not primarily through the word. The child converses with the objects' potential for movement. Rugs are more 'conversational' than fitted carpets, and scatter cushions are more so than those tightly fitted ones that are kept tidily in place with Velcro. A grand piano is infinitely preferable to an upright under which you cannot crawl. A floppy old armchair may be nice to nestle into, but it's chairs round the dining table that convert best into a single-decker bus. And so on.

Equally attractive is the movement conversation that arises if it is the object which inspires the child's *own* movement, such as the nooks and crannies into which you can squeeze to play hide-and-seek, the mattress in the spare room which makes the neighbour's trampoline obsolete, the swinging rope dangling from the rambling old Bramley's Seedling apple tree at the bottom of the garden. When Brueghel painted his *Children's Games* in 1560 his picture reflected the activity of contemporary Flemish children of all ages. Their games required precious little other than the physical body and a wealth of fantasy.

Robbed of our perpetual dialogue with movement in the early years, we become easy prey today for the makers of expensive board and video games (amongst the surrogates of creative play), and of sport equipment later in life, when we find ourselves trying to catch up on our deprived childhood.

If it is some years since one's children have grown up, it can come as something of a revelation to have young visitors who are at the stage of being 'into everything'. Recent research by the UK Kaiser Foundation (October 2003) suggests that television watching and computer games could be damaging the development of young children. The American Academy of Paediatrics has even strongly recommended that television watching be completely eliminated from the lives of toddlers. 'They should be spending time with siblings, with parents and with mud,' commented Harvard researcher Dr Michael Rich. (This was to overlook the targeting of 1-year-olds in order to turn them into toy consumers. I don't think Dr Rich had the marketing of mud in mind!) But although the prime importance of *movement* in a toddler's life was not specifically mentioned in the report, it is clear that deprivation in that sphere is where the 'suffering' really lies. To anyone who does not understand the nature of the age group, however, the advice must appear confusing— spend time 'with mud'!? Indeed, looked at purely from the standpoint of *movement*, of the three (parents and siblings being the other two), and assuming that siblings may not always be on hand, it could well be that mud offers the most potential! But to argue this might be walking on shifting sand, or at least treading on corns!

Earlier, we looked at *imitation* and the spirituality of its wider background. It is this which prompts the child's will to imitate what it perceives taking place in the environment. But spirit and soul in themselves both want the means of outer expression: that is, the physical body's ability to move, with strength in the lower limbs and with amazing freedom and dexterity in the upper limbs. And if you haven't got a Ramon Crater handy, a four square metre sandpit will probably do the trick nicely!

LOWER SCHOOL

Science

'We took a grand piano.'

Reading this, one might with some justification wonder what was coming next. The scene was a Class 6 main-lesson on acoustics. I had been demonstrating how musical tones contain overtones as well as the fundamental, which is the sound that the average listener thinks they are hearing. These overtones are the octave, a fifth above that, the next higher octave and so on. To do this 'scientifically' one can, of course, use a monochord. As the pupils were age 12 and were meeting the Waldorf approach to acoustics for the first time, I decided that, on the basis of science being part of our everyday lives, where possible I would not immediately bring in apparatus from the lab but include the use of as many familiar objects as possible. This entailed our going to the music room where the pupils had seen and heard the said piano each week for some years during their singing lessons. With the lid of the piano raised, the class could all stand around and see, as well as hear, what was going on.

Being Waldorf pupils, and therefore fairly concrete in describing their sense impressions, when asked to write up the 'experiment' during the days following (as part of the so-called three-day rhythm), they almost all included some reference to the short journey from the classroom to the singing room, standing round the piano, removing the cover before lifting the lid and so on. There was only one exception, a pupil who was in the process of making a transition to Waldorf. He was a comparative newcomer to the class who had been brought up in a very scientifically orientated home environment. Not that there was any lack of 'tender loving care'; and he was a boy of heart. But he had already been introduced to a stereotyped way of writing up scientific experiments which started with the formula *'We took . . .'* when describing the apparatus used. Nothing to ridicule, of course, just to *note*, though the surreal vision of taking a grand piano, as if it were any ordinary piece of scientific apparatus from the top shelf of a cupboard in the lab did raise a bemused smile. The scientific approach on which he had been raised, while seeing the truth of the facts, was quite ready to start from the abstract even if it did not exactly accord with the facts—to do an experiment you *take* apparatus (from the lab cupboard).

Of minor importance and therefore discountable? In this case, certainly. But as a training in scientific discipline, it is vital to be meticulous in the pursuit of truth. Steiner's approach to science teaching was therefore what one might term Goetheanistic empiricism or, more simply, *phenomenological*.

It is tempting, of course, once something has been long established as a 'scientific' fact—there is a force which attracts objects to the earth (fortunately not great enough to attract the moon out of its orbit!)—to state the fact and then 'prove' that the statement is true by experiment. Steiner, by contrast, recommended *training the pupils' scientific insight by presenting the phenomenon* and only then getting the pupils themselves to *deduce and explain* what was going on in lucid, rational terms. The method must assume a certain paradigm of course—in this case, limited to the sense-perceptible world. When Diane Conrad carried out her extensive Rockefeller sponsored research into crop circles in 2002, she concluded that they were being formed by hitherto unknown *energies*. Thus her conclusion harmonized with familiar paradigms—the energies were likened to what had caused certain geological formations in past, geological ages, with the astonishing difference that the energies causing the crop circle formation happened overnight (instantaneous?) whereas it is assumed that geological times were long drawn out periods, traditionally measured in tens of millions of years. Thus we have two paradigms which sit side by side: (i) *known energies* (like those connected with certain rock formations); and (ii) the *unknown* (i.e. not otherwise evident today in identical or even similar manifestations).

Prior to Class 6, science does not feature in the Waldorf curriculum in so many words. In view of the fact that in their last seven years at school Waldorf pupils—*all* of them, not merely those who might elsewhere opt for the scientific stream in school—receive an unrivalled, rich experience of scientific subjects, it is difficult to understand how the misconception of Waldorf as predominantly an artistic education arises. There are three possible explanations for this. Firstly, the methodology by which it is taught is Goethean rather than Newtonian, to mention one of the figures whom Goethe thought had got it wrong—at least as far as colour theory was concerned in which he performed and wrote up copious experiments to prove his point. Secondly, the topic doesn't feature on the curriculum *as a specific heading* before age 11/12, unlike, say, gymnastics or handwork. Thirdly, it is assumed that nothing done in Waldorf schools before that age has any significant bearing upon science teaching. Leaving aside that none of these three reasons pursues the matter at all scientifically(!), let us look at what the Waldorf method is driving at. I shall do this by working backwards—albeit briefly—in *three* stages: Classes 6, 5 and 4's studies in minerals, plants and animals, Classes 3, 2 and 1's so-called nature stories, and the activities in the Kindergarten through which the children experience sense-perceptible phenomena.

Stage Three

The main-lessons in which the pupils' attention is directed towards the three kingdoms of nature 'beneath' the human being take place at ages 10–12, that is when their sense impressions are becoming more focused (the study of human biology per se takes place in Classes 7–12). A look at the younger children's drawings will reveal that they are still essentially expressionists to the extent that they draw what they see in the world from a very personal point of view. One shouldn't be surprised to see chimneys rising from the rooftops at some jaunty angle to the vertical, or horses with more than four legs! The attainment of objectivity through perception is a long process.

At first sight, paradoxically, the pupils' attention is drawn to the connection of the three kingdoms with the human being—the *forms* of the various animal species, the *stages of development* of the plants, the *processes* of the mineral world. In fact, the connections illuminate features of the kingdoms in question (outer knowledge through self-knowledge), thus intensifying and making more memorable those kingdoms in their phenomenological aspects.

Stage Two

In Class 1 a genre of narrative is recounted known as *nature stories*. The pupils are told stories about seasonal events in nature that are taking place in the immediate environment of where they go to school. Teachers usually make up the stories based on their observation of form, behaviour or processes in the world around. In the third class, such stories can be purely in accordance with outer reality, and perhaps included in the stories about farming which form an essential part of the curriculum at this age. In this way, they might hear about marjoram, for example, growing around the periphery of a downland wheat field, or about the resplendent autumn colours of the maples and other acers, or the movement of the daffodil buds in the springtime from the sky-pointing way they first come through the dark earth to the trumpet-like gesture with which we associate them, nodding in the breeze on banks of green.

Before the third class, and particularly in Class 1, Steiner suggested introducing some (imaginary) dialogue to the story so that the pupils get a feeling for the inner aspect of the natural phenomenon in question. It is, after all, the inner nature of things that the scientist is eventually interested in, for whatever reason, as well as what comes to meet the naked eye. For example, might not a scientist, who had been schooled phenomenologically, as he glanced up at a bunch of mistletoe hanging from the branch of a tree, have discovered the properties of the plant which can heal certain cancerous conditions had Steiner not got there first? (The anthroposophical medicine Iscador is manufactured from mistletoe.)

Stage One

In Kindergarten, children *experience* natural phenomena through their particularly lively sense perceptions. For example, swinging on a dangling rope offers a range of experiences—the pendulum, gravity, air currents, the flexibility yet strength of the jute fibres (or whatever the rope is made of), the cantilever-like strength of the branch from which the rope depends (an engineering marvel in itself), and so on.

Thus, prior to the long training which the pupils receive in disciplined, scientific thinking (natural *science),* which starts in Class 6, there are the three stages summarized above—nature *experiences* in Kindergarten, nature *stories* in the first Lower School classes, and natural *history* (as it is known conventionally) in the fourth, fifth and sixth classes. What is the educational purpose of the preliminary stages, apart form the fact that they are a joy in themselves *at the time*?

Clearly, all three stages attune and enhance the senses to what they are experiencing. In the paradigm in which contemporary sense perception works, there must be no half measures, i.e. phenomena (unscientifically) overlooked which become the cause of errors, such as drugs getting onto the market which have seriously detrimental side effects etc.

In the first seven years, phenomena are experienced by the senses—as many of the twelve as possible—*unhindered by human intellect* which, by definition, must be limited, for if it were not we would not experience constant signs of intellectual advance as time goes on. These early years give the child a deeply embedded *experience* of the true nature of substances, but at the same time it is *either unconscious or at very low levels of the subconscious* (as with the child swinging on the rope who is most likely simply to be revelling in the sheer movement).

The second phase calls on the teacher to single out a small detail—the proud stance of the oak acorn in the autumn, the dangling clusters of lime blossom in summer, the cheery scarlet holly berries in winter—and to add to the sense-perceptibly factual something of her own which, however imaginary, suggests that there are *qualities* (energies) which are less easily quantified. In this, the teacher's consciousness dwells in an imaginative world. In that respect it is akin to the consciousness of 7/9-year-olds, which is emerging from a subconscious, purely experiential level into a kind of waking dream state (and hence their affinity with stories).

Still greater awareness follows the so-called Rubicon stage of development at age 9 (of which more presently), and this is directed towards the world in the natural history lessons at the third of these stages. The pony, the violet or the north wind remain constants; what has changed, intensified and awakened somewhat is the child's consciousness, which is directed over the course of these years towards the three kingdoms of animal, plant and mineral—animal (living and sentient), plant (living) and mineral (neither living nor sentient).

A Waldorf maxim which is particularly pertinent here is that when the adolescent's thinking embarks on its long path of full awakening it shall be in 'richness of soul'. In the case of science, richness of soul means a wealth of experience of the substances and forces and forms in all the kingdoms of nature that has been gained by the senses *coupled with* the different degrees of consciousness. The outer perimeters of these may be characterized as developing from *maximum sentience coupled with maximum non-conscious empathy* to *highly selective sense experiences coupled with sharply focused awareness.*

We saw that the matter of where to introduce literacy in schools—and for good reasons keeping formal learning at bay—is a real keystone for the Waldorf Kindergarten. Similarly, the carefully and elaborately structured methods that constitute Waldorf science teaching provide a keystone of the Lower School. These two topics stand out in marked contrast to the orthodox methods practised in some educational systems, so they have been introduced here and at the beginning of the section on the Lower School in order to give a certain thrust into the thinking behind Steiner's educational recommendations.

Numeracy

'It's magic.'

The eyes sparkled as he displayed just about the only tooth-complete grin left in the whole class of 6/7-year-olds.

It was our first week of a numeracy main-lesson in Class 1. In groups of twelve the children were taking it in turns to stand in a line and, at the first signal, jump diagonally so that the line divided into two smaller groups of six. At the second signal the line, broken further, revealed three groups of four, and at the third signal, four groups of three, and so on, until all twelve children stood in a long line, with a space around each one. Occasionally we could enjoy a large enough space to not only jump forward but also retrace our numerical stepping stones, i.e. (12×1) (6×2) (4×3) (3×4) (2×6) (1×12) (2×6) (3×4) (4×3) (6×2) (12×1). Having 'practised' the exercise for a few days, we began to get quite proficient, occasionally managing the whole thing with rhythmical confidence and without a single hitch. Nineteenth-century circus-trained frogs could not have been more impressive! It was on one of those successful occasions that the remark 'It's magic' burst forth.

Numeracy in Class 1—'numbers' as it is frequently referred to—is a multi-ingrediented diet of which one of the very first tastes must be *enjoyment*. Every primary teacher (Lower School in Waldorf) knows in advance that she is going to have to jolly along a small but significant percentage of her class when it comes to mathematics, and happy is she if the jollying is well named and not a euphemism for an everlasting struggle, always on the verge of turning sour or—worst scenario—down a one-way street towards maths phobia.

But we will return to this later, for the moment staying

with the eyes sparkling with the enjoyment that number work can be. Whatever else *magic* may mean, it has an element of the inexplicable in it. Until we have sussed out the sleight of hand, the music hall magician captivates a part of us that isn't *only* admiration. Young children who have not experienced thinking as a train of thought that can chug on along a single track for as long as it takes to count from 1 to 100, say, when it comes into the realm of counting are bound to experience the newness of it as something wonderful. They may not realize what the numerical law is (the simplest of arithmetical progressions), but nevertheless they will experience in the flow of words something of the wonder of guaranteed, unbroken logical thought. All maths is, or can be, touched by this wand. Through persisting with such thought processes you arrive mentally safe and sound at your destination—*the answer.*

The affectionate connection with number that pupils in Class 1 can acquire—if that is not too strong a way of putting it—is brought about through developing the plain, straightforward counting in two ways, as is evident from the above anecdote: one through rhythm, the other through movement. Prior to the circus froggy-fun that the pupils were involved in, they had counted rhythmically, placing an emphasis on every other number, i.e. on 1, *2*, 3, *4*, 5, *6*, etc. A few further steps in the same direction leads to the 2 × multiplication table. Similarly, with other multiplication tables: 3 × , 4 × , 6 × ... Thus, they begin to experience and discover that within the sequence of numbers 1, 2, 3, etc. an endless *numerically rhythmical life* can be derived.

Steiner encouraged the multiplication tables to be learnt by starting with the product—*12* = 6 × 2; *14* = 7 × 2 etc.— thus giving rein to an analytical mode of thought in a sphere (number) where it was appropriate at this age. Similarly with number bonds—*20* = 1 + 19; *20* = 2 + 18, etc. This procedure concurs with the maxim *proceed from the whole to the parts*, and inculcates an attitude of mind that seeks the 'whole' to which any phenomenon may be related as well as analysing the further 'parts' into which it may be split.

A more concrete experience of number is brought about through the use of objects which each pupil can handle— Steiner recommended dried beans for the purpose. Given a pile of 24 beans, say, all the four processes (addition, subtraction, multiplication and division) can be brought to bear through a 'hands on' experience. Doing this repeatedly, day by day, alongside other work (the rhythmical counting already referred to, and simple problems presented in image form) leads gradually to the point where the *mental* process takes place without the 'prop' of the pile of beans.

Such a procedure becomes a useful principle for the maths teacher when new branches of the subject are introduced: first give the *outer* crutch for the mind to lean on until the *inner* mental muscles are strong enough to dispense with it. Steiner, in the down-to-earth way that the practical side of his genius often resorted to, referred to this vital pedagogical principle as *getting rid of the beans*.

Only some of the founding principles of Waldorf mathematics teaching can be mentioned here. Another that is particularly potent arises from the fact that the recording of mathematical processes entails becoming 'literate' in a whole new set of symbols. Examples are the signs for the four processes (not forgetting the sign for 'equals'), the shapes of the Arabic numerals (abstract shapes by comparison with Roman numerals), with more and more symbols being introduced as the curriculum proceeds: brackets, square roots, the decimal point, 'places' before and after it, and so on. It is not that such signs are at all complex and beyond reach for the average intellect but that for a child still enjoying the invigorating regime of pictorial consciousness they can appear abstract and remote.

In a very different direction to the abstract—if not arbitrary—use of mathematical symbols is the qualitative aspect of number. It is recommended that children be made aware of this early on in Class 1. This is neither to encourage an interest in numerology nor a retrogressive step towards the kind of arithmetical thought that engaged those in the Middle Ages who studied the Seven Liberal Arts (Grammar, Dialectic, Rhetoric, Geometry, Arithmetic, Astronomy and Harmony). Its principle pedagogical purpose at this age is to give the children who are embarking on their journey into *numeracy* a link with number which is not governed by rationality. A different soul quality presides over qualitative number. Indeed, it can be a gateway into worlds that lie beyond the confines of the 'senses' (resulting in sums that get ticked if they're right and crossed if they're wrong).

From those wider horizons the pendulum swings back from generalities and existential realities to everyday actuality. The teacher invents little problems which the children have to work out. 'Playing' with the beans has made the children familiar with the four processes—how different are the four outcomes of 6 being multiplied or divided by 2, or having 2 added to or subtracted from it! Those are *pure mathematical operations*. Now he or she clothes those operations in outer events and, in doing so, also clothes them in less technically precise (though not less clear) language. For example: 'The daughter of a chicken farmer one day collects half a dozen eggs from the nesting boxes of one of the chicken pens; the family of five are expecting three visitors for lunch; and the mother is going to serve curried rice and hard boiled eggs as main course. How many extra eggs will she need to take from the pantry if she wishes each person to be offered or served with two eggs?' From this information, which the children can picture in their mind's eye, they need to extract the relevant figures and apply the appropriate mathematical process. Thought forms such as the following will go through their minds, though most probably not as symbols.

$$6 = (5 + 3) \times 2 - ?$$
$$6 + ? = 2(3 + 5)$$
$$2(3 + 5) - 6 = ?$$

Incidentally, it is the second of these forms which Steiner considered typical of addition (what must be *added* to 6 to get 16?) where the emphasis is placed on the operation before the figures concerned are encountered!

This brings us into another realm connected with number, that of *reality*—in which one must remain. One would hardly serve a lunch with seven eggs per person! Nor would we collect half a dozen eggs at the end of the day if only two hens used that particular nesting box. The newly ordained curate did not attract respect when he visited the local village school way up in the Yorkshire Wolds and asked the children how many sheep would be left in a field if, out of a flock of 85, seven found a gap in the hedge and went through it. All the hands shot up, almost before he'd finished speaking, and the class chorused 'None'. His chagrin was complete when, after spending some time explaining that $85 - 7 = 78$, a child in the front row with a small voice and a critical eye politely said: 'But Sir, tha knows nout abaht sheep!'

To *express* mathematical reality, however, is another matter. Thankfully we are not confined to Roman numerals (which might even slow down the bright new curate!) where LXXV minus IX would equal LXVI. Thanks to the abstract thinking which came into Europe from Arabic culture, the two eights we see in 808 have very different values because one is in the units column and the other in the hundreds. The teacher will need to devise a pedagogical method that enables the children to grasp this principle firmly, maybe with the help of a story, the images in which make clear what the outer reality is when a number (symbol) moves from one column to another. If the principle has been well learnt it will provide an ethical basis for carrying over (multiples of ten) from the units to the tens column in multiplication or division (e.g. 5 × 13 or 17 + 34) or for converting tens into units when we move in the opposite direction in subtraction or division (e.g. 45 − 18 or 868:7).

Reading about mathematics teaching is not everyone's idea of fun or magic, so I will call a halt at this point and move on to the next topic. One certainly cannot expect the fascination of number to be universal. Nevertheless, the *educational* benefits are incalculable. With technology insinuating itself further and further into the playroom, the bedroom, the bank, the airport, and into our very friendships, we do well to pause from time to time to take stock. The *time* we save not having to fell trees to provide warmth on a cold winter's night we may well make good use of elsewhere. But technology (in the form of the calculator, say), 'saving' young children from developing their thinking power, comes into a completely different category. In fact, it is not a saving but a *deprivation*—one which causes lifelong disadvantage. Joy, therefore, in an activity which has far-reaching consequences for the wholesomeness and quality of each individual's life is vital. And if that joy bursts out in an expression such as 'It's magic', *so long* as those Waldorf maxims are firmly in place, which Steiner identified as being of core value for the developing child, who are we to quash it?

Inner Perception: Memory

'Be quick!'

The house lights had hardly been dimmed 30 seconds before the 7-year-old in the front row, with a voice like the commander of a team doing fire drill, called out.

Not that nothing was happening. The occasion was a performance of a staged version of a fairy tale which the teachers of a Rudolf Steiner school were putting on for the school community. The pianist was setting the mood for the opening scene (let's not call it an overture), as formally requested by the director; the magic of blue and scarlet lights played on the great wine-red folds of the front of stage curtain. But the atmosphere that all this combined to weave and conjure was lost on the sandy-headed lad. As had other children in the audience, he had been told the story of the play. But in him the anticipation of seeing what by now had come to reside in his memory was at bursting point, and he couldn't wait for the curtain to go up. His belief in the magic of the scenes to come needed no assistance from lighting or music. Full of matching the past with the future, he only wanted to twin his life-size memory of the story with what was about to happen on stage—that is twin *inner* perception (memory) and *outer* perception as the action unfolded, and in the process experience the invigoration of it all.

The response from the pianist had its amusing side, for he shot like an arrow from the bow to the theme which was to have been played towards the very end of the improvised curtain-raiser—an agreed signal to those back stage to start opening the curtain. Taken somewhat by surprise, players scurried into place. The person opening the curtain jerked herself out of the relaxed mental mood into which the music had transported her, the prompt promptly flipped to page one of the script . . . and, like the characters springing back to life at the end of 'Sleeping Beauty', they were off!

When speaking to teachers in June 1920, Steiner explained that *memory* was an inner activity similar to the act of perception which takes place via the senses. Usually the intellectually active mind works so quickly that as soon as we see the bus for which we are waiting heave into sight we are hardly engaged in our sense perception of the bus *per se* any more. We are gauging the distance it still has to go before it reaches the bus stop; we are checking we have our return ticket or our travel card in hand ready to show the driver. If it's a request stop, we are anxiously watching to see if the bus is slowing down in response to our outstretched arm. As it gets near we are wondering how full it is and looking for signs of passengers standing that would indicate whether we will get a seat. But we are most likely not contemplating the exact hue and proportion and shape of its familiar roof or bonnet. If it were surmounted by a baby giraffe nestling beside its mother we might get precipitated afresh purely into our senses, at least for a moment! But we'd probably soon become intrigued by the surrealist impression made, or enjoy remembering our infrequently fed concept of 'giraffe'. Occasionally in life we see something which is unrecognizable for a sufficient number of seconds for us to *remain* in our perceptual activity. Perhaps it's on a family photograph and we find part of our consciousness in a 'blank' state before we realize that the background behind an object is, say, the bark of a plane tree. Note that: blank. It is the *thinking* mind which prevents the percept from having its say.

This is of enormous importance for the educator, whatever may be their educational philosophy. Although fortunately it is not the only way of assessment, most examinations (the results of which become an entrance ticket to so many careers) consist of means of ascertaining whether the candidates 'know their stuff'. To take a crude example, better that the surgeon whose anatomy is somewhat wanting is sifted out at the examination stage than that later he has to bury his serious mistakes!

Leaving aside (perhaps with a degree of envy for some) those people with so-called photographic memories who, having looked once at a page of some obscure legal point, can retain it for life, leaving aside such minds and focusing on the age group of childhood with which we are at present concerned, the teacher is constantly faced with the question of *how* to present something so that the child retains it. We have all been in the situation where we need to communicate with someone who is deep in conversation. Their mind is engrossed in their subject and their senses are drinking in the nuances in the other's voice or picking up subtle facial expressions. We are seldom poker-faced as we speak. In such a situation we tend to obliterate other impressions. Nothing in our peripheral vision registers. Thus the one needing to communicate either interrupts ('You're needed on the phone,' 'Your child is crying') or tries to *catch the other's eye*. Having done this we gesticulate as emphatically and concisely as we can: ('Time to go,' 'You're spilling your sherry,' 'There's no sign yet of the Dunstanburgh-Campbells!' 'I urgently need the car keys').

With luck the teacher may not be competing with the child's attention being riveted elsewhere—though it is wise to be aware that anything can 'walk' into the classroom. Nevertheless, she *is* competing with the future and the demands that it will make on the child's memory. She therefore needs to know not only how to *catch* attention but, like the ancient mariner who waylaid the wedding guest, how to *hold* it until she has finished telling her story—and in such a way that after the wedding guest has shaken out all his confetti and multi-toasted the bride and groom he will have clear access to the memory of the mariner's escape from death's sharpened scythe.

What are the skills the teacher will need to do this? Like the ancient mariner, she will need to have something worth saying (it goes without saying!) and she will need to have communication skills. But however epic-like her Epic may be narrated, the listener has to have a potential interest in it, a potential that can be maximized by her storytelling acumen. Thus the teacher will need insight into the nature of the child, both so that she can determine her curriculum and also so that she can develop the pedagogical method by which she 'delivers' it. This is the keystone of the archway which denotes, perhaps, the most significant understanding of Waldorf and its intimate connection with *child-relatedness*.

Though Steiner had much to say about the curriculum it was at best secondary to what he had to say about pedagogy, and that in turn was completely driven by his communicating in ever deeper detail his insights into the nature of the human being *in childhood*. Anyone who describes the Waldorf curriculum as 'prescribed', as happened in an article in the *Times Educational Supplement* in November 2003, is about as far off the mark as they could possibly get. *Prescribed* suggests a finite body of knowledge. The closest Waldorf comes to that is in the 'science' of understanding child nature, though the boundaries determining that knowledge seem to be capable of ever being extended, as teachers soon discover when they imbue themselves with that knowledge. Indeed, as they revisit Steiner's expounding of child nature—an essential ingredient in the life and discipline of teachers—they are more than likely to gain insights of their own. Then, in a creatively working Waldorf school, they will air their developing understanding in faculty meetings (the Waldorf equivalent of a research cluster) where insights can be discussed, fine-tuned, corroborated, opposed, resolved, in a healthy spirit of collegiality.

This body of knowledge is to teaching what colour is to the painter, what pitch, rhythm and harmony are to the composer, what fabric and form are to the dress designer, and so on. In a word, it is the knowledge needed for *art* to communicate; and that art is pedagogy. One might say—though this is stretching a point—that the school curriculum is the *result* of the artistic pedagogical activity of the teacher who is well informed about the nature of the child, just as the picture on the gallery wall is the result of the painter's skill or the bureau the result of the furniture designer's skill, who could well also be the cabinet maker.

An unauthenticated Ghirlandaio *pietà* is not going to fetch the same price at auction as the real thing just because it's a *pietà*. The value lies in the master's hand. Likewise, the value of education lies in the pedagogy, for that's where the skill that reaches the memory of the child lies. Were that not the case, all that education would entail would be for the curriculum to be couched in the most lethally dry terms, devised in some office far away from the classroom, and for the child to be flip-charted through it—and everyone would be queuing up for double firsts at Oxbridge.

To put it crassly, after a superb meal, the feel-good factor is very different from what we swill down the plug hole before putting the dinner plates into the dish washer. The feel-good factor of education needs to last a lifetime—and results from only one educational meal (which lasts for one's whole school career). But it's how we paint the *pietà*, how we navigate the *Titanic*, how we conduct ourselves after our imprisonment on Robin Island that counts, not the curriculum that was long ago swilled down the plug hole of our schooldays. And all those 'hows' depend on those things that—apart from our skills—have resided in our memories, and whose permanent residence there depends upon the pedagogical expertise of our teachers.

We are reminded every Armistice time in November, one way or another, of the nightmare memories of soldiers caught up in the trench warfare of the Great War—about as diametrically opposite to child-friendliness as anything could be. Though the vast majority of today's population have been spared that, we all have indelible memories of something that thrust itself into our lives, such as a surprise visit, finding a banknote, meeting our partner, flying over the Alps. Every schoolday in a child's life brings something from outside— not as a life event in an adult's biography, perhaps, but nevertheless as significant, either in the realm of skill, value-acquisition, attitude-building or simply plain knowledge.

The teacher's pedagogical ability, though transformed, enables us to access what we need in our memory. *And ideally those memories need to be capable of growth and metamorphosis.* At one end of the scale we will have the power to raise the curtain quickly to perceive what we urgently require from it. At the other end, we may find it worth listening to the music of life for a while so that we bring to what we hear as the curtain of memory lifts qualities that mingle with our memory perceptions and make more of them than they originally contained. In contrast to this, a prescribed curriculum, 'delivered' and its delivery *inspected* (see again the *TES* article quoted above) to ensure that the prescription is dished up to the letter, is the certain death of a living pedagogy—indeed, an anti-image of true Waldorf.

Etheric vs. Astral

'His rage was wild to see.'

It was a Class 1 play. The reaction at the back of the hall was a unique cocktail of emotions. The wee laddie who was 'acting' the part of Rumpelstiltskin was standing front of stage, with his classmates clad in costume in a crescent moon shape behind. The teacher had decided that the spoken parts should remain in chorus throughout so that all children identified as much as possible with the whole story, but that it would be a pedagogically sound procedure for each child to wear the costume of one of the characters in the play that she had written, based on the original Grimms' fairy tale. This had the double virtue of each child possessing the story in the form of rhythm and other poetic elements, while also witnessing the events of the story—either through co-creating or through looking on—via a succession of tableaux.

It was wonderful to be in the audience, to experience the children so fully enjoying both roles: being part of the chorus and acting. They won the hearts of the whole school. And that was what created a dilemma for the Upper School adolescents, which in turn gave rise to what I have called a cocktail of emotions. For the boy who had been chosen to play the part of Rumpelstiltskin had probably never experienced rage in his life. He was clearly imitating what he had seen the teacher demonstrating as everyone chorused, namely, clenching her raised fists and, with something approaching despair, shaking them violently, before plunging her foot into the ground and disappearing, never to be seen again. Good pedagogue that she was, in order only to convey the *image* of rage (these were 7-year-olds), and not the inner astral turbulence that it induces, or from which it stems, she had shaken her fists in keeping with the rhythm of the words. Her pupil had 'translated' this into a kind of fisticuffs ding-dong in which the raised forearms went up and down in gentle alternations, while the hands slightly see-sawed in between.

Hence the conflicting emotions wafting down from where Classes 8–12 were seated at the back of the hall. Full-heartedly they took in and responded to the human situation, no doubt in some cases with endearingly nostalgic memories of themselves way back in Class 1 welling to the surface. At the same time, the pure outer reality of rage of such a Rumpelstiltskin from an astral perspective was incongruent, to say the least, which pushed them to the very edge of self-restraint. So while the younger classes took the passing image in their stride, all as part of their appreciation of the colourful spectacle of a class play, a wave of suppressed guffaws was followed by a moment of embarrassed adolescent silence, in which they mused whether their reflex reaction had over-stepped the boundaries of even adolescent decency.

Adolescent decency! A grey area indeed, but not only grey! Though it may not seem at first particularly very close to the classroom, since we began with the concept of *rage*, let us continue with it to help ascertain the essential difference between the 7+ pupil and the 14+ young person. In other words, if we are looking primarily at the former, what are those qualities that are important to emphasize and, perhaps in certain circumstances, what are those qualities that essentially belong to a later stage of development? Steiner broadly characterized the 7+ stage of child development as being presided over by the *etheric* (life forces), while the 14+ stage is one in which the *astral* forces become dominant.

All anger is not necessarily of the flew-into-a-rage type. This already suggests a lack of control. When we overhear a conversation in which the voices in the next train compartment increase in loudness and the 'narrator' declares: 'By this time I was boiling . . .' and if the train has arrived at the station where we get off, we will be left in the dark. Did she allow herself to boil over? Or did she hold back—*take herself in hand*, take herself off the boil?

With this example, we have actually extended our consideration beyond both the 7+ and the 14+ stages of childhood to the adult. As adults we know what it is to fly into a rage—with various reactions: 'I feel better for that!' 'I can't think what possessed me!' or simply 'I'm sorry.' Equally we know what it is to 'channel' the anger into a positive deed. This might be expressing how we feel in a sufficiently objective way to be of benefit to the person who has occasioned our anger. Even at the moment when we are aware of the spark igniting, the ego may be able to exercise sufficient power to contain itself and prevent the astral flaring up.

With the ego not being in command to the same extent in adolescence, control in such situations is unlikely. Subjectivity tends to reign. We are not speaking of ill will but simply the condition of adolescence in which the soul's more powerful emotions are no longer cushioned by the etheric (more plastic) nature of the younger child nor yet tempered by the maturing ego of the adult. A skilful teacher will find means of directing the adolescent's propensity for strong emotional (astral) reaction to worthy causes. An even more skilful teacher will do the same thing for *opposite* causes, such as that which impelled both Cavaliers and Roundheads, so that the adolescent recognizes that there is justification on *both* sides, and that while historically they 'lost it' (the monarch Charles I being perhaps in the most ignominious position in this respect!), given greater wisdom or diplomacy the conflict might have been otherwise solved.

With the 7+ pupils, the Waldorf view of things recognizes of course that anger is a constituent of the soul, but it does not incite the pupils to the point of feeling the rage as something personal. However strong the anger is, it is attached to the *outer*. This is not the same as what we term objectivity. The picture of anger—'His rage was wild to see'—is not the same as the personal experience of it, even if that experience is on behalf of (or in sympathy with) a third party.

Through schooling the inner life in this way, we build a bridge between the developmental stage of the first seven years—when anger can be described simply as an external expression of the organism (a 2-year-old throwing a tantrum)—and the adult whose ego is in control. As Blake put it: *I told my wrath: my wrath did end.*

And the same goes for other soul qualities, though clearly some are more amenable to being brought under control than others—something which can vary considerably from person to person. Cravings, whether they be coffee or smoking, do not possess each one of us to the same degree, and they therefore present us with different degrees of challenge if we decide to discipline them. A five-hour gun battle between rival drug cartels somewhere in the world suggests a vastly different degree of astrality to that which has instigated a five-minute discussion on the radio between right and left protagonists of some minor political diversion which the media has brought into prominence as some slightly fanciful stocking-filler in the 'silly season'.

Thus, the educator attempts to strengthen the life forces of the 7/14-year-olds. Music and movement are examples of subjects that lend themselves to this. Let us look at music, trying to reduce its complexity into simply graspable components, to shed light on this procedure.

Music is an art, a 'performing' art. It contains elements which are organized in a particular way. A *scale* consists typically of seven notes whose relative *pitches* are related in a mathematically ordered way. The *length* of each note bears a relationship with the length of the others, through which arises *rhythm*. The rhythms are ordered into groups; each group is marked by a very slight dynamic emphasis, which is referred to as *beat*. The notes are ordered in such a way that their respective lengths, combined with their relative pitches, produce phrases, which are referred to as *melody*. When more than one note is heard at a time the combination is ordered so that it sounds *harmonious*. Successive harmonious sounds are ordered so that an aesthetic experience results, which is the more 'professional' meaning of *harmony*.

The human soul possesses the musical ability to perceive the above order. Indeed, over the millennia it has created it. In childhood this perception is first schooled *actively*. From Class 1 onwards the children both play and sing music. The music in which they actively participate therefore permeates the soul. And as the 'repertoire' builds up over the years, the music becomes ingrained in the soul as an ordering, harmonious, aesthetically satisfying source of strength—strength that is commuted later into one of the discriminative powers of the ego. This is a power that can be called upon and exercised by the ego whenever the astral (soul) forces come into play. Thus music (amongst other things) endows the soul with strength for the future. The archetypal image of this in Greek mythology is Orpheus with lyre in hand, taming the beasts, an image which Schikaneder (the librettist for Mozart's *The Magic Flute*) replicates in a somewhat pantomimed fashion.

Having distinguished various aspects of the astral forces, let us return to the central features of the middle classes (ages 7–14), the 'birth' and nurturing of the etheric through education. Especially since we have identified Rumpelstiltskin, and can therefore temporarily leave the astral forces of raging adolescence, are we in a strong position to do so.

Bridging the Child's Journey from Spiritual to Earthly Realms through Narrative

'I loved that story.'

It was on a busy pavement one Saturday morning in 1965. Christmas shoppers were bustling by. It was not quite the end of term, however. My friends with their daughter who had been at the birthday party of my 7-year-old the evening before were merely round and about on a routine weekend shopping jaunt. The parents renewed their genuine appreciation expressed the evening before, while I looked down at the small girl. You could see from her somewhat distant gaze that her consciousness was still in some other 'space'. Fun danced in her eyes. But there was more. And then, in a little lull in the grown-ups' exchange, out it came: 'I loved that story.' There had been party balloons, of course, and plenty of noise, but as it drew towards the time for the parents to collect their children, we had organized a story round an open log fire in warm, subdued candlelight. The excitement of pink icing and party games magically evaporated as the simplest of the Grimms' fairy tales—which many of the children must have already been familiar with—wove its images throughout their gladdened souls. And here was the echoing wonder of fairy-tale-land sparkling in the inward-dreaming eyes of a 7-year-old on a street corner as we met casually, stamped our numbed feet and tightened our scarves in the biting wind.

As we saw in an earlier chapter, Steiner was emphatic that it was just as important to contemplate pre-existence and nurture an open-minded attitude towards it as it was to nurture the positive feeling that many people in his day had towards the after-life. Childhood is the major stage on the journey of the human spirit from its spiritual to its terrestrial home—the process of incarnation. Never mind if the concept is somewhat vague at first (how could it be otherwise?), the deep-down conviction of the reality is what could *inspire* the educator in his or her work. Inspire—that is to build a bridge across which the human spirit can enter wholeheartedly from pre-existence into earthly life, endowed with gifts from the past and motivated to meet the destiny which still lies in the future.

Leaving aside what 'gifts from the past' may mean, there are clearly two aspects to the educator's task. One is to find *the means* of building this bridge and the other is to give the incarnating human spirit sufficient *encouragement to cross over* it with the assurety that participation in earthly life is vital if evolution is going to progress, and if, in progressing, it will really tackle some of the problems that cause humanity as a whole to be its own worst enemy.

Whether we take a Gradgrind view of education and consider such an aim to be a luxurious and therefore entirely optional auxiliary or whether we place the aim on equal terms to knowledge can be discounted here. It is not a case of 'whether', but 'assuming so: how?'

One of the most convincing answers to this 'how?' can be found in the narrative material recommended for Classes 1–5 in the Lower School. In Class 1 the three main genres will be found referred to as *fairy stories, nature stories* and *pedagogical stories.*

Genuine *fairy stories* are something of an enigma to many modern people. The term itself is often used colloquially to mean downright untrue. 'Don't come here with those fairy stories!' 'Fairies are figments of the imagination and are not to be mentioned in the same breath as plastic credit cards, hip replacements and weapons of mass destruction.' This stern dismissal of the genre obtains in some quarters despite the fact that only a minute proportion of fairy stories have any creature that is or even resembles a fairy—indeed, the name of the genre in other languages mostly does not incorporate anything to do with the so-called fairy world, something that becomes plain if one compares their mood, say, with what Shakespeare conjures up so convincingly in *A Midsummer Night's Dream.*

But worse is to come. Not only are fairy stories an enigma, they are a source of veritable irritation to those who are out to expunge any trace of sexism, ageism or racism from society—and no doubt there will be other 'isms' in plenty to witch-hunt. Certainly the images that occur in fairy tales have to be seen in a certain light if they are to be above that charge.

What is that light? It is that everything in the fairy tale— including all the characters and creatures, all the landscapes and weathers, all the likelihoods and unlikelihoods—are mirror images of what is to be found to one degree or another in the nature of *each human being.* If we cannot recognize the ailing king, the princess and the old wise woman in our-selves—as well as the spinning wheel, the gloomy wood, the babbling stream, the iron stove, the glass slipper, too—then we have simply not yet penetrated the images sufficiently to discover the universal human reality which they encompass. Those realities disclose how, behind all our personal traits and idiosyncrasies, there are elements which are the absolute hallmarks of our humanity, our humanity in so far as we are connected with the evolutionary flow of time, in whose current are to be found all ages and all peoples. The fairy tale encapsulates through its imagery the human being's place and role in our present epoch vis-à-vis the vast panorama of evolution. The inroads which the several interpreters of fairy tales have made in recent years, though seriously significant, do not appear to be frequented much. One must simply press on towards the self-knowledge which the fairy tale offers.

The so-called *nature story* is unique to Waldorf. It focuses on something in nature which is to be observed at the very time of year that the story is being told. The object (say a snowdrop in winter, if it is in the northern hemisphere, or an agapanthus in summer in the southern hemisphere) is not brought into the classroom, as might be the case in an 'object lesson'. At the same time, the story will encourage the children to take note of the plant when they next see it outside. The story will focus on a detail, from which the *quality* of the object—not necessarily always a plant—can be gleaned. It embodies the teacher's attempt to penetrate through the sense-perceptible phenomenon, ideally in a Goethean sense, to the spiritual reality which is the creative energy behind the object. Colour, gesture, ecological environment, texture, time of year, scent, form—any aspect of the plant that helps the storyteller, in dwelling upon it, come to a deeper understanding of its nature can be taken into account.

That understanding is then converted by the teacher into an imaginative dialogue between the object of the story and something it comes into contact with, or which lies in the vicinity. The dialogue is indicative of the fact that the object has life and is not merely a dead piece of mosaic in some vast picture of a world that can be explained purely in material terms. The nature story thus builds a bridge between the confines of earthly space and the infinite which we associate with 'other worlds'—those worlds from which life stems in all its abundance.

There is a third element in this bridge-building process connected with the narrative in Class 1. This is embodied in the *pedagogical story*. As a genre it is related to the so-called remedial story and has to do with human *behaviour*. 'The Little Boy Who Cried Wolf' is both widely known and the perfect example of its type. It describes a nuisance trait in the mischievous boy which, in spite of all the efforts of the neighbouring villagers, he makes no attempt to curb and which leads to its logical conclusion. For when the real wolf does actually appear loping onto the scene, despite the boy's now despairingly genuine cries of 'Wolf!', it gobbles him up together with the feast it makes of the newborn lambs in the flock that the boy has been tending. The only difference between the Waldorf pedagogical story and the remedial story is that while the latter was told for general entertainment but with the purpose of cultivating an ethical way of conduct in a bygone social setting, the former is directed, though not overtly, to a specific individual.

When first coming across Steiner's recommendation that such stories be told, people often find it difficult to understand. Questions arise such as: Might not the child's enjoyment of the mischievous behaviour depicted in the story backfire? or: Won't the child for whom the pedagogical story has been created feel crestfallen in the stony silence that invariably ensues after the sad ending, his self-esteem possibly even permanently punctured? or: Surely it is the 'love' of the teacher that is going to be the remedy, that is going to prompt the child to sweep clean the hitherto neglected dusty corner in his being?

There is no doubt that *loving concern* emanating from a child's teachers is a supportive element in the child's development and can be a vital factor in progress. In the pedagogical story it merely takes on a different form. In the everyday situation the child experiences the loving concern in his feelings (albeit probably somewhat below the threshold of consciousness). Despite what must arise from time to time as reprimand, it is there as an abiding factor. In the pedagogical story the teacher strives, through her creativity, to address the child's higher self—a member which is as much above the child's threshold of consciousness as the feeling-centred awareness of his teacher's loving concern is below it. The story could be regarded as therapeutical.

The image by which this shock treatment (if you like) is conveyed has the chance of working positively rather than counter-productively because (a) at the *end* of the story there is no *redemptive* element—the redeeming feature in the genre is, as described above, that as well as everything else she is doing the teacher makes the effort of creating such a story; and (b) the *disguise* element in the story (e.g. the child in question for whom the story is told is a girl not a boy, and her father is a stockbroker and not a shepherd), together with the fact that the *whole* class hears the story, removes any threat of the kind of public exposure that is part and parcel of the day's work on other minor reprimand-like occasions.

Thus, the higher nature of the child is encouraged to cross over the bridge to where their earthly life has its home, and this invariably causes with it improvement in the child's whole demeanour. Whilst, in this instance, the child is unlikely to say, 'I loved that story,' gratitude for what brings about improvement is an equally important virtue.

Narrative in Class 2

'Oh no, not again this year!'

Christmas Plays, which have become well known through being performed by many schools in the Waldorf Movement, were 'discovered' on an island in the Danube by Steiner's Professor of German Literature, Karl Julius Schröer. Known as the *Oberufer* plays, after the island where they had become part of the folk tradition of Christmas celebration, they form a trilogy. As one might expect, there are two plays depicting the visit of the shepherds and the three kings to Bethlehem—based respectively on the accounts in the Gospels of St Luke and St Matthew. These are preceded by a short but dramatic play showing the Fall of Man from Paradise. The plays are usually produced by the teachers towards the end of term as a Christmas gift for the children. It was on the occasion of seeing the Paradise play for the second time that a child called out the above, obviously having identified with the error which she considered Adam was making in taking a bite of the forbidden fruit.

To borrow from biblical imagery, it would be true to say that the genre of the fairy tale spans in metaphorical form the whole of evolution from the Garden of Eden through to glimpses of the Apocalypse. In the quaint story form in which the fairy tale is couched this is deemed appropriate for the pupil in Class 1. Within the same framework of biblical imagery, it would be fair to compare the fact that, on the one hand, while the Gate of Paradise was closing inexorably, on the other hand the Divine Powers are in the long term benevolent and that they had placed within the human being the ability to restore what had been lost (though in a completely different form). Reverting to the past is not on. Future generations will have to fashion their own approaches to morality.

In Class 2 images in the narrative genres bring home (a) the fact of 'loss'—the closing of the Gate; (b) that the seed which has been planted within the human being, however long it lies dormant, can be germinated towards future development; and (c) the realization that spirit powers, in so far as they await man's call for help, are effective.

Humanity's weakness in giving way to temptation—those moments when we behave one-sidedly or primarily out of self-interest, or when we have simply 'lost the plot' finds quaint expression in the *fable.* Fables are mostly concerned with animals. 'The Ant and the Grasshopper', 'The Fox and the Crow', 'The Sheep in Wolf's Clothing', 'The Fox and the Crane', etc. are amongst the more well known of Aesop's collection. In these stories we are shown how, in contrast to the 'integrity' of the animal species, which is embedded in each creature's bodily based *instinct,* the parallel trait in the human being is branded as something very definitely beneath human dignity. Language is full of expressions that refer to the *animalistic tendencies* in our behaviour—even if this may seem a strong label to attach to our peccadilloes: a bull in a china shop (insensitivity), sour grapes (lack of magnanimity), cunning old fox (given to using intelligence in tandem with unsavoury guile), and so on.

So that the children maintain a joyous and caring respect for the animal kingdom, as good pedagogical practice, Steiner recommended instigating an exchange of news and views in class, *before* the teacher relates the fable, about the animals which are about to feature in the fable. Such an exchange also gives the opportunity for the children to become conscious, even if only at a faint level of feeling, of the corresponding animal quality in their own souls. In this respect, the snake in the Paradise story is the representative of all one-sided animalistic tendencies to which we are subject as part of our human heritage.

In the same year, stories about *saints* are told, which are aimed at making the children aware in their feeling life of those human beings who have blazed a trail. We don't have to call them saints, of course, and by so doing run the risk of limiting the choice of stories we wish to tell to one particular ethnic tradition. In such accounts the children experience that, if not as yet in humanity as a whole, there are and have been people who have overcome their lower nature, their one-sidedness, their antisocial egotism and the like, achieving thereby powers—wisdom, healing, guidance, blessedness, relieving poverty, and so on—which are universally recognized as beneficial for the society in which they lived and worked.

These impressions from fables and so-called saint stories are further complemented in Class 2 by legends being told in which the benevolence of Divine Worlds breaks into ordinary daily life. Such legends are often concerned with the miraculous (e.g. a harvest is saved from severe drought, a fishing boat with its crew is saved from a merciless storm, a lost traveller is rescued from the wilds, a supernatural sign of some kind affirms the innocence of someone supposed guilty of a crime) and are usually connected with actual places. Every shower of rain, at the right place and time and in the right amounts contributes, of course, to saving a harvest from drought. While such things are something to be grateful for, in the legend a situation is encapsulated that is distinct from the normal course of Creation's benevolence. The divine succour that is depicted in the legend is *in response* to a situation in which the people concerned cry out for help where they are in peril or some other form of adversity.

One could say that, at this stage in their development, the children are pointed towards a vista of the future—*their* future—in which human freedom increasingly prevails. That freedom offers the possibility of recognizing and calling upon 'higher powers'. But in it lurk the dangers of our falling from grace, though there is also the possibility of each one taking himself or herself in hand and making something meaningful and positive out of their lives.

In terms of the Paradise story and its reflection in the Class 2 narrative genres, one might say that all that leads to the moment of Adam's biting the apple one could connect with *fable*; the hurling away of the apple when Adam realizes what the consequences of his action are likely to be indicates that the forces of self-redemption are born, i.e. that which leads to *saintliness*. And Jehovah's endowing Adam and Eve with the 'gifts' or faculties they will need in the earthly life that results from their fall from the paradisaical state can be connected with *legend*. Not only 'this year again' but always.

Narrative in Classes 3, 4 and 5
Its Significance for the
Child's Changing Consciousness

'My father doesn't believe that holy people have horns.'

As part of the ongoing narrative venture in Class 3, I had brought along a postcard showing Michelangelo's *Moses*, one of his colossal marble sculptures which is situated in San Pietro in Vincoli, a church near the Coliseum in Rome. The protuberances that Michelangelo carved above Moses' temples had obviously made an impression that was deep enough to prompt some remark round the supper table that evening. Yet it was hardly the kind of feedback I had been anticipating!

The reason that Steiner gave for including the Old Testament stories in Class 3 was that the book was outstanding amongst *world literature*. It is not that Waldorf wishes to convey any one-sided impression that Judaism is based on something that is super-monumental. There is plenty to be found in Waldorf that directs the pupils' attention to the spiritual foundations of different ethnic groups across the entire globe. Religion lessons themselves are free of sectarianism. Indeed, I doubt if a richer educational curriculum in this respect could be found. Hearing the stories in such a comprehensive work narrated, nurtures understanding of another people—if not in the same measure as studying a modern language over many years, at least in essence. In Classes 6, 7 and 8, the warmly sympathetic pursuit of such spiritual roots in any given situation (e.g. Bosnian Serbs, Australian aborigines, the indigenous Incas of Peru, Canadian Inuit or the Hotentots of South Africa) may take little more than one or two days of main-lesson time since there is so much else to cover in the curriculum. Yet in those short periods of time, the pupils will receive abiding impressions that cover a large part of the spectrum of the human race.

In Classes 3, 4 and 5, Steiner pointed to three outstanding mythological historic traditions, Hebrew, Nordic and Greek, the narrating of each one to be spread on and off over a whole year. The Hebrew legacy corresponds to the echoing on of the division in the innermost voice of the human soul. The Nordic legacy (here the *Edda* is preferred to its Teutonic equivalent on which Wagner built his mighty tetralogy *The Ring of the Nibelungs*) corresponds to the increasing dependence upon the individuality, stirring within the human being, in the light of Ragnarok, the demise of the Gods of ancient Valhalla. The Greek legacy—a mythology whose images are very far removed from the everyday reality around us, both in respect to relationships and incidents—is one which stands at that point of human development (ontologically and philogenically) where philosophy and therefore literature were born out of the experiential realities that lived behind the mighty panorama of mythological images.

People with modern consciousness will not readily arrive at the truth behind the images in mythology—even if someone like Michelangelo has paved the way by giving Moses horns to indicate his spiritual supremacy, or if from ancient Greece sculpture after sculpture of, say, Hercules gazes down at us from plinths in museums or reliefs on the entablatures and friezes of temples. From this point of view, the teachers who are recommended that mythological stories have educational value for children will be at a disadvantage. But that disadvantage will soon be outweighed by the healthy appetite that the pupils have for such stories, for in turn it will prompt the creativity of teachers as they develop their insights into the wisdom that lies behind the puzzling—often bizarre—images put forward.

Later in the Upper School opportunities will occur to return to those images and bring the light of the pupils' developing rational thought to bear upon them, as did the Greek philosophers themselves. In the Lower School, the two faculties are nurtured somewhat separately. The mythological panorama keeps the child's picture-making and pictorial sense-making alive. Food for *thought* itself is provided by topics such as arithmetic and grammar.

In addition, in the fifth class, a third faculty is awakened in the child's changing consciousness: *the building of the bridge between the two modes of thinking (pictorial and intellectual).* There comes the realization that understanding of outer images can be derived through a rational process. This is brought about in two related yet distinct ways. One is through the study of plants, and the other through the study of the 'archetypal' beasts: eagle, lion and bull.

From the pedagogy employed for the teaching of botany in Class 5, we may deduce that Steiner attached particularly special importance to it. The circumstances were his discussions with the teachers designate in the first Waldorf School in Stuttgart (August 1919). He wanted them to come up with a good suggestion, but they were only partially successful, despite taking several days over it. He finally elaborated the method himself, which in brief is as follows.

As the teacher describes each plant group, going up the scale of evolution from the 'lowliest' fungus to the 'loftiest' dicotyledon, parallels are drawn with the human being. The comparisons between the animal and human kingdoms which are drawn in Class 4 concentrate purely on *form*: the elephant's tusk, the pig's snout, the horse's hoof and in each case the human bodily equivalent. In Class 5, the comparison

enters into the element of *time*, being about how the 'use' of
the body reveals the soul-spirit nature of the child as incarnation takes place.

Comparisons drawn between the three beasts—eagle, lion
and bull—and the human being go further. From the visible
(the sleeping baby in the cot, the toddler, the adolescent . . .)
they move to the invisible, that is, the child's attention is
drawn to its own inner soul qualities. After describing the
outer characteristics of the eagle, its habitat, the way it
plunges towards its prey and so on—perhaps in the days
following, looking at other birds too—the teacher then
discusses with the children what aspects of their own thinking
are similar to those characteristics. Similarly with the cat
family (lion, tiger, puma, panther) parallels are sought with
the life of feeling, and with the bull—and, of course, the cow
and other ungulate species—the parallels are to be found in
the activity of the will.

In both the above examples a bridge is made between
outer nature and some aspect of the human being. Visible,
though not directly present in the classroom, except for the
11-year-old stage which is where the children are at, is the
development of the human being from birth through to
physical maturity. Invisible, i.e. accessible only through the
child directing its gaze inwards more consciously than ever
before, yet at the same time present there and then in class are
the soul's three powers of thinking, feeling and willing.
Michelangelo clearly thought that forces were contained in
Moses that merited outer expression if his outstanding nature
was going to be understood. Thus he carved the horns on
Moses' forehead in the region of the temples. They could be
said to represent the inner forces the human being needs in
order to become ever more acquainted with, and in command of, life if it is going to succeed in becoming self-
directed and purposeful.

As to what we believe 'holy people' have or what they don't have—perhaps we can leave that one safely stewing . . .

The Rubicon

KEEP OUT OF REACH OF CHILDREN
I was lecturing in the north of Scotland and was accommodated in a room that had only recently been vacated by a former Waldorf pupil—the youngest member of the family to fly the nest. Most of his belongings had been extricated, but there were still books in plenty. The temptation to peep being too great, I was scanning titles on spines on one of the top shelves when I came across a book that had been covered with brown paper (the only one, in fact). With increasing curiosity, I took it down and found the front covered with the kind of bold red label you'd find on a bottle of some lethal sink-cleaner in a hardware shop: *Keep out of reach of children*. Carefully peeling off the brown paper wrapping to see what the book was about, I discovered it to be a *German grammar*!

The ninth/tenth year, the *Rubicon* as Steiner frequently referred to it, is one of the most distinctive stages in the whole of child development. It is the age at which the *self* in terms of self-consciousness takes a significant step forwards. The term Rubicon itself derives from the name of a river near Rome. It is usually used to denote 'there's no going back'— and that is certainly the experience of many children at this age. Not that one should think of the 10-year-old as a mini-adult. Nevertheless, some aspects of childhood are most definitely becoming things of the past at this stage, and are likely on occasions to be uninhibitedly scorned by the rest of the class if they get a whiff of such a lingering trait in a classmate.

Here I shall look at the developmental situation via the metaphor of a river *valley*. As one approaches the river, one *descends* down one slope; and after crossing it and leaving it behind, as the river threads its way through the valley onwards, downstream, the other side of the valley presents an *ascent*.

Similarly with the child, the 'descent' towards the ninth/ tenth year leaves the peaks of early childhood behind and the ascent presents new challenges. But one should not think of the descent as necessarily the easier of the two. To descend a mountain slope means that there is minimum gravity to overcome, pulling against you. But the descent from the peaks of childhood means that—for want of a better word— the *spirituality* of one's early years becomes ever more distant. Thus as children approach the Rubicon years, alongside the joy of coming into the richness of the valley there is the feeling of loss of the past with all its abounding spirituality which has been such a support and an encouragement hitherto. For the educator, this will often mean awkwardly unpredictable affronts which call for firm but tactful (classroom) management.

At the same time, the educator's role is one of compensation. As the spiritual support of the past starts to fade, the child needs warm-hearted *human* support in its place. This, however, cannot be expressed in any gushing way that would cause undue embarrassment in the advent of the Rubicon child's greater self-awareness.

In this, Waldorf teachers have, in the suggested curriculum, topics which give the child encouragement to make the descent towards the valley below. The Old Testament mythology-leading-into-history has already been referred to. Through the unrivalled richness of the episodes contained in its 'books', the children experience how humanity (albeit embodied in the historical past of the ancient scriptures) suffers the expulsion from a paradisaical state, as well as many tribulations in its subsequent journey, but is nevertheless not forsaken by its deity (in this case Jehovah). At a spiritual level this represents some recompense for humanity's self-ostracization from the divine presence.

Secondly, the bodily needs of the human being are provided for by what are described in the Oberufer plays as the 'goodly fruits of earth'. History shows how the way that the fertility of earth was husbanded, changed from the mere taking (when we were gatherers or hunters) to a form of agriculture in which human intelligence cooperated in a sustainable way with nature (when we became cultivators, *farmers*). This epoch-making transition is indicated in ancient Persian scriptures. In a series of main-lessons, usually broadly referred to as 'farming', this grandiose vision for human survival is experienced in miniature by the children. Thus, not only is there spiritual recompense for humanity's fallen state, but also the wherewithal to nurture the physical body.

Our well-being requires still more, however. This 'more' is represented in main-lesson blocks devoted to the place that *house-building* holds in society. While farming provides us with our *daily* needs, the provision of a house is much longer term. Outwardly the house provides protection from the vicissitudes and excesses of climate. Inwardly it means we possess a space for personal development, which has been constructed with natural resources but designed and created and formed through human skills. These skills, moreover, have become specialized to the extent that they are provided for the individual by the 'community' of builders—following the architect, the bricklayers, carpenters, plasterers, electricians, etc. with a mutual recognition of need in the form of the flow of money. The purchaser pays the landowner, the builder, the architect and the lawyer. The builder pays the bricklayer, the glazier, the plumber and other subcontractors. The brickyard owner pays the electric company (if that's how the kilns where the bricks are fired are powered). The electric company pays the colliery (if the material used for the power generated is coal). The colliery pays the miner who has laboured down the pit. The miner pays the baker who provided the bread for his sandwiches, and the other retailers of provisions. The baker requires an extension building and seeks tenders, including one from the builder who paid the bricklayer, who purchased the bricks from the brick-making firm, who . . . . No wonder 'The House that Jack Built' has set going some trains of thought over the generations!

Thus, in Class 3, the pupils descending towards the Rubicon experience through these main-lessons great pillars of support for their new situation in life. The spiritual is still there for the one who feels the need and has the will-power consciously to cultivate the connection anew (the silent message from the Old Testament). The everyday nutritional bodily needs can be met by cooperation with the forces of nature, particularly in the animal and plant kingdoms, and where those forces are transformatively at work in the soil and weather (the silent message from farming). Dwelling places are constructed using mainly the mineral resources of the earth; by providing dwelling places each personal soul can develop and can discover its own richness and ways of cultivating that richness not only for its own good but also for that of its fellow human beings (the silent message to be derived from house building).

The above provides the child with the beginnings of new inner strength, new inner confidence, new security. Moreover, the lessons are all taught using pedagogical methods that are appropriate for the age—unlike the German grammar, they are well within reach of children! They are then ready for Class 4, which is much about confirming the budding self-awareness engendered *through challenge*.

Affirming New Self-awareness

'D'ye ken anything aboot the past, the present and the feuture?'

I was standing at a bus stop in Aberdeen, surrounded by the grey granite buildings for which the city is famed, when a wee laddie—around 10 years old—lined up beside me. Was it that I looked as though I had all the time in the world to spare (standing in a bus queue can make you feel like a tiny speck in a very captive audience)? Or was it that he was simply boiling over with excitement at what he'd been hearing at school? Perhaps a bit of both. Unless you know something about the age-related nature of the curriculum in Waldorf education you wouldn't be very likely to conclude that the branch of grammar that goes into the broad division of *tenses*, into past, present and future, would be likely to bring a child's enthusiasm for learning to boiling point. One also has to bear in mind that this was not only a sandy-haired, pale-blue-eyed Scot—the Scots being reputed to be *thinkers*—but he was also an Aberdonian. Aberdeen has been mildly but nevertheless pointedly boasting for over half a millennium that England was not the only place in the British Isles to have *two* universities in the fifteenth century (Oxford and Cambridge); *it* also had two! I was aware of this, but had not been expecting the extramural arm of university life to extend quite as far as a 10-year-old at a bus stop!

Steiner considered the study of grammar to be particularly beneficial in the activation of the inwardly turned life of thought. Most people acquire at least the rudiments of the grammar of their mother tongue before memory dawns. We can probably think of half a dozen instances of 3-year-old chatterboxes either coming a grammatical cropper (which only serves to highlight that most of the time they canter along at ease with this aspect of the mother tongue), or inventing the grammar they need to make a point. I am reminded of the child who wanted to emphasize that he had remembered to wash his hands, despite his mother's persistent questioning, and who being at his grammatical wits end protested: 'Yes I did; I *doneded* it!' The raising of those rudiments to consciousness, and the ordering and refining of them, is what gives strength to the inner self—that inner self to which autobiographical memories are so intimately attached.

This topic already begins in Class 3 with the parts of speech (verb, noun, adjective, etc.), taught with a very child-friendly approach. It continues throughout the Lower School, eventually culminating in Class 9, at which point no sentence becomes too complex to be grammatically unravellable by the 15-year-old's awakening intellect.

The relationship of this inwardly perceived self to the outer world also requires affirmation. This is done through a concentrated study of the locality, in which the child can begin to discover how human beings through the ages have worked with and changed the face of nature. Through the narrative of what people have done locally and, as a result, left their mark on the landscape—roads, bridges, tunnels and tracks, place names, inns, police stations, cemeteries, buried shards of pottery, imported non-indigenous vegetation, harbours, reservoirs and waterways, trades and industries, hospitals, monuments, quarries, houses, castles and places of worship, etc.—the children get a feeling of (a) being part of a *community* which strove and throve in the past and which is still active (albeit with changes); and (b) *their* particular abodes, home and school being the centres of the locality, at least as far as their own ego is concerned. This is irrespective of what the future may hold. Thus, *the self, vis-à-vis the stream of humanity through the ages, with reference to a particular locality,* is what this main-lesson is about. There are usually two blocks during the year, and the title most often given to it, Local Geography, though approximately flagging what is going on does not hint very adequately at what hides in the depths. Local Geography-cum-History would perhaps be nearer the mark. But as with so much of Waldorf, this offers yet another opportunity for the teacher to be creative—anything, one might say, that brings Waldorf alive and combats the grossly mistaken concept that the Waldorf curriculum is prescribed.

The reciting of alliteration is said to strengthen the feeling of the independent self. Northern epics (such as *Beowulf* or the *Edda*) offer good examples, but there is other poetry from pre-Chaucerian times. The searching teacher may sometimes be rewarded by discovering something that has local relevance, such as the poem which celebrates the blacksmiths who smelted iron in the Forest of Anderida: Swart smirched smiths smattered with smoke,/ Drive me to death with the din of your dents, etc. In the south, the home of the hexameter, measure is all. Short and long syllables—and we still tend to refer to the syllables of northern, Germanic languages as short or long—are precisely that; a short syllable takes a shorter time to pronounce than a long one. This is illustrated by the well-known line *Caesar adsum jam forte; Pompey aderat*. The contrast of the northern mode, in which language consists of emphasized and unemphasized syllables, is further illustrated by the mischievous metamorphosis of the above, howler schoolboy fashion: *Caesar aderat forte; Pompey had a dormouse!* To gain effect, the first clause is spoken in southern style, i.e. with measure:— - — - — - —. The second clause gains in impishness if the mode of speech is switched to emphasis:— - - - - — —. Even *Pompey* sounds comical in this context, let alone what follows.

But although the shift in the 10-year-old's taste for humour is an important factor with pedagogical implications for classroom management, we are in danger of diverting from the question: Why alliteration?

To recite with the attention focused on measure, which has been the keynote hitherto in the school, has the tendency to lift language from bare meaning into a kind of soul-music. Nursery rhymes spill into song more readily than into speech. Classes 1, 2 or 3 reciting more often than not 'lift' the poem into a kind of song-song, which brings out the lyrical beauty of the language, like varnish on wood brings out the beauty of its flowing grain. In the extreme, it almost denies the essential emphasis/non-emphasis quality of the Germanic-based tongue. But plunge into alliteration and you swing the pendulum in the opposite direction. The repeated consonantal sounds cluster in the ear—but it must be genuine alliterative poetry—none of your GM-alliterative so-called tongue-twisters. They have their place, of course, in foreign language teaching, but in the mother tongue we are pre-eminently in the realm of *art*, a realm absolutely central to the 7/14-year-old's whole experience of 'growing up'. The emphasis which the repeated consonants necessitate in alliterative verse calls on the ego. While something like hexameter lifts language into soul-music, alliteration, like the eye of a mini-linguistic hurricane, spirals the ego down into artistic consciousness.

Hurricane? At first hearing, it sounds an inappropriate image for the ego. A lighthouse guiding the mariner through the stormy ocean might be more appealing. Though an analogy must not be taken too far, of course, the advantage here of a hurricane over a lighthouse is that it moves. And in moving it makes its mark, which admittedly can be destructive. Nature needs to restore her beauty if she has been uprooted or dishevelled, and this happens generously in Class 5. Yet we need constantly bear in mind that the ego in human development is something of an oddity. As with the nursery rhyme 'Mary, Mary quite contrary', the ego is not like the other three members—physical, etheric and astral—set out like 'cockle shells, and silver bells, and pretty maids all in a row' in the garden of child development. Contrariwise, it comes and goes in fits and starts. Like waves building up to a climax on the shore of life, it makes itself felt in advance. It heralds its own advent, particularly at the Rubicon time we are considering. In the past, through imitation, it drank in the supposed goodness of humanity. In the future, it will strive towards idealism and truth. But in the present it needs a temporary anchor in the harbour of beauty.

Thus, in the light of the foregoing, the teacher of 10-year-olds could do worse than to ask himself: *D'ye ken anything aboot* the ego, *in the past, the present and the feuture?*

Gaining Self-confidence

'How high shall I draw the sky?'

The question came from a newcomer to the class. He was about 10 years of age like the rest, but was making the transition to Waldorf. Most questions asked on public platforms about the transition between Waldorf and mainstream focus on moving in the opposite direction, and invariably they are in connection with things like the three Rs. This is entirely understandable in view of the assessment mania prevailing in many mainstream settings—though happily in Wales (and hopefully at some point in England?) brighter horizons are surfacing.

But what of the child himself? Does it matter where *he* is at—or how high he feels he might like to draw the sky or anything else for that matter in his picture?

Had the question come from one of the 'old hands' in the class I would perhaps have thought it rather pathetic, or that the child was feeling 'off colour'. Here, however, it was the clearest indication I'd had since admitting the boy into the class of where he *was* at. Firstly, he was certainly more abstract in his thinking than a Waldorf-schooled 10-year-old—with the 'how high' question indicating the downside of this—a weakness in imagination. I suspect he had missed out on the vigorous, participative degree of consciousness of young children who live predominantly in their will and will-imbued feeling. This meant that the story he had heard the day before had registered but not been avidly digested. When children of this age are let off the leash to draw creatively, there is no hesitation as to the main figures in the picture and what goes where. They are not inwardly looking *at* the picture they are drawing, like a landscape painter might be;

normally they are *right in it*. As they draw, heads down, they unhesitatingly take up one crayon after another in what can appear like a veritable heat of creativity. Often, simultaneous with putting down the last crayon, they are on their feet bringing their creation to show you, seeking your comments, seeking affirmation from the one who is their authority in the arts.

By contrast, *drawing lessons*, per se, are not spontaneously stimulated by the inner life. The type of drawing I have been describing is the child's inner response to what they have heard narrated the day before, carried so to say through sleep—carried, enlivened and elaborated—which inner experience they now are eager to externalize (using crayon, paint, clay or whatever medium is available). The drawing lesson per se does not concern these inwardly active processes but calls on the senses. An object is put before the children or their attention is drawn to something already there, which *there and then* they are asked to draw. No time or opportunity is given to subjectifying. The result is as free of the subjective as possible, i.e. it is *objective*—the object is drawn objectively. What the *eyes* see, the mind and *hand* translate into a two-dimensional drawing.

The skills for both types of drawing—the 'free' picture and the 'copied' object—derive, of course, from the same source: the ability to put crayon onto paper and move it in a controlled way, thus making marks/forms that show some sort of likeness. But the psychological routes are by no means parallel.

Before Class 4 Steiner emphasizes the importance of form drawing. Out of, and at the same time guided by, an experience of movement (which can involve the whole body), the hand 'traces' on the paper an image in miniature of the form drawn by the teacher on the board. Such form drawings—lines following and manifesting certain patterns—

make the child conscious of form per se. When order is brought into movement, patterns arise: one line 'moves' in a wavy, horizontal fashion; another moves with right-angular precision, like the pattern on the hem of an ancient Greek tunic, and so on. Through such form drawings the children become conscious of a wide spectrum of form: angularity, verticality, diagonality, acuteness, obtuseness, steep and shallow curvature and a host of others.

The consciousness of 'form for form's sake' thus aroused and enjoyed is directed, starting in Class 4 to the forms in the outer world before later entering the world of pure geometry. A line is drawn in a certain way, but still freehand (compasses and straight edge come into service in Class 5), making a square or an oval or a trapezium. Looking at the outer world, I discover the forms that I have come to know in my form drawing, e.g. the spokes of a wheel ray out in circular fashion from a common centre (the hub) to the periphery (the rim); the chest of drawers appears as a number of interrelated rectangles; an old farm wagon will combine such elements; and so on.

What I merely experienced—played with, shoved around, climbed on, gambolled over, slid down etc.—in Classes 1 and 2 and earlier, I discovered in Class 3 could be measured (had a certain depth, longer or shorter sides, or if it was a wheel it had a measurable perimeter and diameter). Now in Class 4, I take that step in my relation to the outer world, making it more conscious by putting on paper its image (albeit still not exactly to scale). The child's *impression* of it is still valid—as you can see in his drawing which is fancy free—but *it* also has validity.

The Rubicon faces the child with the world. Before this stage children experienced themselves as simply part and parcel of the world. They tumbled and romped and swung and skipped and paddled and built castles, dens and tree-houses, revelling continuously in will-involvement. Now they begin to *know* that they are distinct from the world, however much they are also active—galloping on horseback or swimming or somersaulting... And that process of self-knowledge continues—through painting with colour perspective in Class 5, through becoming aware of the way light and shadow play on surfaces in Class 6, through further exercises in linear perspective in Class 7, through surveying in Class 10, through ... through... The senses become ever more acutely schooled in their perceptions of the outer world.

At the same time, the *self* has a commensurate need for schooling in its self-perception. In Class 4 the three great divisions of time, as manifest in the past, present and future tenses of verbs, support this self-perception. In round singing (canons and quodlibets, too), through the challenge of increasing self-reliance in the realm of singing music (which is very much an inner realm), that self-perception is further strengthened.

A child with such strengthened self-perception—which pervades his whole nature, filtering and diversifying into qualities such as self-expression, self-esteem, self-confidence and the like—when given the opportunity to draw a picture of a story he has heard the day before will not be dithering, sitting before a blank page dubious about how high he should draw the sky. With psychological sleeves rolled up and muscles flexed, what he does will almost certainly not be what you or I or his neighbours will be doing. But, be it high or be it low, *he will be busily getting on with it.*

Anthropocentricity

'Come and see what Alex has got!'

It was a large box for a 10-year-old to be carrying. The wood itself from which it was made was solid—a pre-war cabinet-maker's job—heavy, even without the contents. Followed by a flurry of his friends, the boy who had been inspired by our main-lesson to bring this piece of family treasure-trove to school came into the classroom with an expression which revealed a mixture of physical strain (the school car park where he had been dropped was some distance away) and excited anticipation. His friends were obviously in the know, judging by the grins on their faces; and the rest of the children, sensing something was afoot, were being drawn in like floating leaves into a whirlpool.

The huge box was placed ceremoniously on the floor—inwardly ceremonious, that is, but outwardly somewhat plonked down due to the relief of getting rid of the unaccustomed weight! An incongruous and slightly comical movement. After a few remarks which further fanned the flaming excitement, I gingerly lifted the lid. The silence that fell over the clustered crowd of children was an intense contrast to the buzz that had crescendoed so far, as I saw staring up out of the box—with the children torn between looking at the macabre object and glancing towards me to observe my reaction to it—the deathly white skull of a hippopotamus. It was difficult to find one's bearings between the shattering polarity of gross ugliness and the awe-inspiring beauty of this 'word' of creation. (Following 'Let there be light!' from somewhere amongst the chorus of Elohim, presumably there must have resounded a 'Let there be hippopotami!') The mood it evoked certainly presided throughout our entire main-lesson that Thursday morning—though I noted with quizzical amusement that, at the teachers' meeting later in the afternoon, where I had reported the unique incident and exhibited the skull (feeling, I have to admit, as I opened the lid of the box, a bit like a music hall magician), when it came to the school doctor's contribution to our child study, with thinly veiled Germanic pointedness, he asked for the lid to be replaced.

The main-lesson followed one of Steiner's suggestions for the age, to study the *animal world* by comparing the outer form of some species with that of the human being. This is far from being anything like the comprehensive view of zoology which is usually scheduled for Class 12, but the method does reflect the anthropocentric nature of Waldorf education. Common choices amongst Waldorf teachers include both wild and domesticated animals (e.g. the mouse and the horse), but it was not Steiner's intention necessarily to remain in the sphere of the familiar. His description of how to teach about the cuttlefish makes that clear. Even dwellers in a sea-girt isle are unlikely to have experienced a live cuttlefish down on the sea bed; and the Swabian children in the first Waldorf school, some 85 years ago and hundreds of miles from the nearest coast, must have been even more in the same boat!

The aim of the lesson, therefore, beyond general knowledge, is for the children to experience how *specialized* the animal's bodily nature is (serving the group-soul's bodily implanted instinct, if one wishes to take a swipe at the behaviourists by putting the horse firmly before the cart!), beside which the form of the human body is *reserved*. While enjoying the way our Tarzan appears perfectly at home swinging amongst the apes, or while cheering on our Olympic gold medalists as they sweat on the racing track, we do also look for some truly human attitudes at the end of the day. We even expect civil behaviour from our soccer stars and thump them on the media and in the courts if, off the pitch, they don't conform to decent standards. The hoof and agile limb of the horse, the otter's deep-set incisors, the snuffle-potential of the pig's snout—to the artistic eye, all manifest each of their 'owner's' essential nature, even if they are only viewed in glass cases in the natural history museum.

Human beings have forgone such specialities in favour of *flexibility*—despite Tarzan's biceps, the published 'statistics' of last year's Miss World contestants, the sensitive fingertips of a Braille user or the highly developed taste buds of a vintner. Nowhere is the reserve more manifest than in the form of the *human hand*. Even if we had organized all the baboons in the Western Cape 'bashing' on typewriters ever since the machine was invented—and even if one of them *had* come up with a line from *A Midsummer Night's Dream* (and surely no one would envy the regiment of quantitative researchers wading knee-deep in paper while frantically checking the results!)—the creature's 'hand' described in the research when finally appearing in its refereed academic journal would still need inverted commas to differentiate it from the real thing.

But though we are blessed at birth with the reserved form of our hands, it is some time before we are able to put them to the supreme creative use for which their potential is destined. The schooling of the hand is one of the keynotes of childhood. Back in their cradles, the hands of Leonardo, Paganini, Florence Nightingale, or any Palestinian housewife who prides herself on making falafel must all have revealed, however delicately, the creative impulse which we call play. Each act of play calls for the hands to trot a little way down the road along which one or other of the animals has galloped full tilt—be it the extinct dodo (do we know what they *did*?), the dam-building beaver, the nest-weaving weaver bird, the ice-loving penguin or some animal, maybe, that has not yet been discovered in the wilds of Papua New Guinea. Could it be that the toddler's swift change from one activity to another and her joyfully impulsive demolition of the tower of wooden building blocks she has just built tell us: No, the hand is not a tool for building or for anything else, though I can use it for that; the hand holds back so that it can *join hands* and 'build' the future of Earth evolution.

When it comes to the fifth class (age 10/11), the start of this human journey is charted by comparing the *evolution of the plants* with the main landmarks of child development: from crawling to standing, to walking, to speaking, to thinking and so on, until full pubescent maturity has been reached. The bodily development thus followed offers a dwelling to the incarnating individuality and finds its counterpart in plant evolution, though it would be too forward at this early age to liken the incoming individuality of the human being to the ability of the plant cells to absorb what they require from the light and the nutrients taken up from soil, water, and air—differentiated as this ability is in liverwort, seaweed, moss, conifer, spring bulb, fern or orchid, etc.

In the same year, Class 5, as mentioned earlier, further analogy to human development is pursued through studying the three time-honoured archetypal families of creatures: *eagle, lion, bull.* Through learning about the eagle's attributes (other birds too), and the lion's (together with other felines), and the bull's (alongside other ruminants, bull *and* cow), analogies are drawn which help the children become more conscious of their *inner* life of human thought, of human emotion, and human will-power—though it would probably be going too far to expect the 11-year-old to appreciate all the constant and complex interplay of these three soul forces.

Pursuing further the anthropocentricity of Waldorf

education, the beginning made in the early classes is carried forward into each year, though it is possible here only to touch on the main themes. The principle is also found in subjects not directly related to natural history or the sciences—it is all-pervasive.

In Class 6, using the categories of intrusive, sedimentary and tertiary *minerals* as analogies, the bodily *functions* of threefold human nature are broadly alluded to: the nerve-sensory, the respirative-circulatory, and the reproductive-metabolic. This opens the gateway in Class 7 through which the human being can be seen from a more subjective viewpoint. Hitherto the perspective has been essentially objective: the outer human form, the increasingly incarnating individuality manifest in children's early achievements, the inner life reflected in the three soul activities of thinking, feeling and willing, and the three 'systems' just referred to of nerve-senses, etc. In the Class 7 main-lesson that is often referred to as 'Health, Hygiene and Nutrition', the children are faced with those variables which have their cause in how we behave. Health, hygiene and nutrition broadly imply wise conduct of life, something which is even more evident in the adjectives healthy, hygienic, and nutritious. A 13-year-old is only too aware—and pedagogically can be helped to become still more acutely so—that we humans can and do get tempted into things that are unhealthy, that we can and do slip into the unhygienic, and that we can and do indulge in the inadequately nutritious or the non-nutritious. Thus the curriculum offers an opportunity to connect the objective—and *why* something is healthy or hygienic or nutritious entails an *objective* study of the corresponding aspects of the human bodily functions—with more *subjective* considerations, with moral issues arising as we nurture the body, in the way we behave, in our lifestyles, in the habits we form, or, failing this, if we are pulled in directions that undermine, bombard, damage or abuse it.

In the remaining five classes, further topics that have a bearing on human biology reopen these two doorways—the facts of human nature and how we respond to them—through main-lessons on the twelve senses, anthropology, embryology, psychology, etc. Finally, in Class 12 a birds-eye view is sought. From studying comparative religions (with their norms and dogmas from the past) and philosophy (the evolving starting point of human behaviour) and their impinging on the practicalities of how we conduct ourselves, the pupils gain a new, objective vantage point—the broadest possible, wherever circumstances will allow. This can enable them to determine how they are going to use their about-to-be-conferred freedom when, having left school, they become increasingly the directors of their own lives.

In the final analysis, from the wonder of the *given* (the hippopotamus skull etc.) extends the long road of evolution leading to the wonder of the *achieved* (Kew Gardens, the Taj Mahal, the Sphinx, Dante's *Divine Comedy*, Rodin's *Burghers of Calais,* Handel's *Messiah*, Monet's *Water-lilies*, the common zip, a medicine for cancer, etc.). Provided that the right education has been achieved—and here I am broadly presenting Steiner's case for an *anthropocentric* approach—the crossroads to which that long road has led, at which each 18-year-old stands as he or she prepares to step across the brink of freedom into life, will include, broadly speaking, the humanistic way. The mechanistic and the fantastic will, of course, always be there fulfilling certain needs in life. Wise travellers will not neglect these. But there will be a good chance that, at the same time, they will not lose sight of, indeed will return to, the 'straight and narrow' (not at all in any narrow, pinched or diminutive sense), the open way *reserved*, shall we say, for truly human progress.

Heart Knowledge as Part of the Emancipation of the Astral Forces

'It's wot I luv uvver people wiv.'

The scene was an open air school in Euston Square, London, after the First World War. Think away the menacing overhead swoosh of jets coming into Heathrow and replace it with horse hooves still clopping on the cobbles!

I heard about the incident through a colleague who had taught in the school for a time. It was mainly young teenagers from disadvantaged homes who attended. My colleague, who was straight out of teacher training college, had been introduced to Steiner's thought by two senior lecturers. They ran a study group one evening each week on Steiner's pedagogy for those who were interested. In those days one could hardly have expected his philosophy to have filtered into any formal mainstream programme: (a) it was a 'system' still in process of being established, and (b) between the strong stream of spirituality that ran through it and the theory and praxis of the 'establishment' the gulf was still to need some decades to be bridged. Indeed, the bridging is still going on in many quarters, with gaunt, ungainly and unfinished cantilevers jutting forlornly into the sky of educational theory.

In those study groups one of the main things that held professional appeal to the 20-year-old students was the depth of insight Steiner invariably sparked off into the nature of the young adolescent, many of whose extreme moods and reactions they were going to have to deal with in the climate of comparative social chaos which was one of the irksome legacies of the war. The cockney adolescents whom she taught in Euston Square, on the one hand, were about as streetwise as anyone under the sun, but on the other hand, within their emotional turmoil, often lashed into tornado intensity by some brawl outside the pub at closing time the night before, there was a sensitivity that bordered on purity and, dare one venture to say, innocence.

The remark above came in response to an opening gambit the teacher had used one day: *What is your heart?* Untrammelled by notions derived from popular potted science, and aeons before the internet and TV had invaded the thinking of youth, without any hesitation one of her girls came out with it: 'The 'art Miss?—well it's wot I luv uvver people wiv, ain't it?' ('Silly fool, not to know a basic fact of life like that,' almost implied by the tone of voice!) A quarter of a century later and that scene was as fresh in my colleague's mind as if it had been yesterday. It had confirmed for her, right at the chalk face, what those lecturers of hers had pointed out from the Waldorf approach, which supplemented the orthodox view of adolescence as that stage of childhood where the intellect reigned and therefore was the teacher's prime, cram-in-knowledge responsibility. Or to put it more radically: here was a newly graduated educationist, trained to presume to be streets ahead, learning basic human psychology from the streetwise!

The whole truth—in fact, perhaps the *key* to understanding the young adolescent (age 12/13), still on the childhood side of twice-seven years—was to understand the deeper, less reachable, less fathomable aspects of the soul. Steiner spoke of the emancipation (even the 'birth') of the astral organization. My colleague's way was via the heart, language to which she rightly believed her neglected, disadvantaged, abused, old-before-their-time girls would relate. She was proved correct. So her lesson went on—a string of lessons threading through the ensuing weeks, in fact— exploring *the landscape of the heart*.

At that age 12/13 in a Steiner school, a main-lesson is taught entitled 'Wish, Wonder and Surprise'. Its external aim is to improve the individual's creative writing; its inner educational aim is to enhance the individual's awareness of the vast richness that lies waiting to be discovered within the human soul.

But why wish, wonder and surprise, rather than, say, doubt, exhilaration and modesty or any other triad of soul moods you care to pull out of the hat?

Wishing, being engrossed in wonder, and being taken by surprise can be seen as three qualities that delineate the broad horizon of the soul's inner landscape. When *wishing*— whether for egotistical reasons or altruistically, whether frivolously or with deep yearning, whether positively or maliciously, whether subjective or objective, personal or impersonal—the process begins by the wisher becoming aware of a lack of some kind, outer or inner. This develops into a wish to make good the lack, though it does not necessarily get translated into deed. Even if it does—adding an accessory (say a handbag of a particular shade of carmine) to one's Christmas shopping list—there is no *guarantee* that the wish will be fulfilled. While occasionally we feel 'stuck in a rut' and find ourselves vaguely wishing something would come along to haul us out of it, mostly our wishes are specifically directed: the relief of famine in Ethiopia; a prayer that a friend might recover from an illness; a mounting anxiety that the 'baddy' in a movie be apprehended. What-ever the wish, it begins from a point of awareness that awakens within, followed by a gesture of going out—be it tentatively, rapaciously, beseechingly, temptingly or in some other mood—towards the object of desire *but without guaranteed fulfilment*.

The gesture experienced in *surprise* is essentially polar opposite to this. Something comes from without into the soul and has a definite origin: the baby sneezes for the first time; the circus clown produces a trombone from out of his baggy trousers; we fail an exam we were expecting to be a walkover; our car comes unexpectedly to halt short of colliding with the lamp-post towards which it was skidding on the icy bend; the Council Tax for the year has not been increased; we solve the latest knotty problem that life has presented, to everyone's satisfaction. In each case, though in different degrees—a surprise can be as gentle as a midsummer dawn or it can whiz in like a mosquito after you've turned out the light—the soul is taken aback. Often the breathing gives away what is going on: we laugh at the punch line of a joke; the spectators gasp in sun-hat-clad chorus as one of the tennis players trips on the centre court at Wimbledon; we hold our breath in suspense as the unanticipated horror piles on blood and thunder in a mystery thriller, and so on. Straight away, after the surprise, the soul has to deal with whatever it is that has invaded its 'space'—hurtlingly, insinuatingly, jocularly, disparagingly. The adjustment may be as quick as a shrug of the shoulders or it might take the best part of a lifetime to come to terms with.

Between these two soul gestures, indicated by the terms 'wish' and 'surprise', is that corresponding with *wonder*. The soul moves towards the object of wonder—it may be enduringly, disbelievingly or just 'lost' in beauty. At the same time, the object of wonder—which has claimed the wonderer's attention, despite a dozen other phenomena which might have been competing for it—releases, as it were, some of its attributes. These might enter into the wonderer as knowledge or simply deepen the aesthetic pleasure being experienced. Whichever it is, the wonderer consciously gives space to what is emanating from the perceived object while *simultaneously* intensifying and directing the senses. As distinct from wish, however, the soul gesture going out in wonder is *terminated, is aimed and arrives* at the object or some detail of it (the graceful movement of a giraffe's neck, the size of the hands in Michelangelo's *David*, the blaze of brass instruments that opens the last movement of Beethoven's *Fifth Symphony*, the hair on the wart on the nose of the wrinkled old moneylender in a Dutch genre painting). The simultaneous gesture—from without entering into the soul as with surprise—is also to be distinguished from surprise in that it is not invasive. In wondering, we *deliberately* open our soul so that the object of wonder may 'speak' to us. We endeavour to gather in as rich a percept as possible by being open-minded, given up to what streams towards the senses.

The above is an attempt to describe the three processes going on in the exploration of our inner life. How we may bring them to the children's awareness is a pedagogical matter and is therefore the business of each teacher, Steiner education being non-prescriptive in essence. But whatever pedagogy the teachers use or develop, the aim will be the same in all cases: to help the children become aware of the *full horizon* in the landscape of the soul and, at the same time, all that exists in the near or middle distance, the happy, meadow-moist plains, the terrifying precipices, the majestic peaks, the murky forest shadows, the streams and dikes, the marshes, the volcanic cones and all the morphological wealth that images what lives within the human soul.

But there is still more on the teacher's agenda: having made the pupils aware, he or she has to lead them further and help them cultivate ways of expressing that awareness, mainly in the creative language of the mother tongue, but also perhaps in painting, or mime, or improvised musical expression. This second part of the process raises what might otherwise easily subside back into the dim realm of feeling towards discerning consciousness, thereby implanting in the adolescent a faculty that can be drawn on to enhance both the boundaries of knowledge and self-knowledge.

When we speak of 'affairs of the heart', we are usually referring to relationships of some kind. But the cockney adolescent in Euston Square after the First World War was clearly more universal in the way she thought of the heart. And if something *rings true* coming from an unknown East Ender, it is surely just as valid as from some acclaimed authority who has a long list of published titles to her name.

Economy of Teaching

'Yes, we're right in the middle of it.'

I was visiting a solicitor in Bristol. A Green Paper had been issued by Parliament concerning institutions providing for special needs children. It followed on the heels of one of those increasingly frequent cases of abuse having come to light, causing serious ripples throughout the system which end up washing on the shores of legislation. The law lords tighten the screw to deal with—preferably pre-empt—the worst scenario. So everyone feels the legal pinch, which is expressed in ever-mounting heaps of paperwork and less freedom, less time to devote yourself to the needs of those unfortunates whom the law purports to protect. And there is the uncomfortable feeling that behind it all is: Trust no longer prevails; X, Y and Z betrayed it; and A–W shall all suffer the consequences as well. Although I had had some seven years' experience of working in the special needs sector, it had been more than two decades earlier, before I had retrained as a Waldorf teacher. I was merely called in, on this occasion, in a consultative capacity to help prepare a formal response to the paper.

The long hours we spent with our heads together were relieved by supper. The meeting took place in the solicitor's home rather than at his office; so supper was not only a welcome break, it was a very enjoyable family occasion. The youngest member of the family attended the local Waldorf school, and on discovering that he was in Class 2, I asked him what the class's main-lesson was. 'Fables,' he said, with obvious delight. So I continued: 'Have you had the story of "The Lion and the Mouse" yet?' At this his delight ignited into unusual eye-sparkle: 'Yes,' he replied, and added, with much emphasis and a gaze which showed that although he sat at the supper table his whole being was wrapped in a kind of reverie elsewhere, 'We're right in the middle of it.'

Now a fable must be one of the world's shortest stories— *The Lord of the Rings* or *War and Peace* in the minisculest of molecular nutshells, so to speak. So although chewing of supper and other topics of conversation prevented further exchange on the subject, my curiosity was roused. Indeed, my thoughts are still frequently drawn back to that moment. What does it mean to be 'right in the middle' of a story that takes less time to tell than it takes to boil an egg? The case is even more extraordinary if I add that this was Friday evening—a whole weekend in fabulous suspense!? Yet clearly his spontaneous reply couldn't possibly imply that the teacher had broken off the narrative at some point, invented a cliff-hanger in a narrative that is no more than the size of a badminton court in the gentlest of undulating countryside. Conceivably, it might have meant that he or she was rehearsing a playlet on the theme; I was too bemused to think of enquiring. But whatever it was, I cannot recall a more substantiating example of the Waldorf maxim: Determine the best topic for the age and teach it with the right pedagogy, and you will rouse optimum interest in the children.

Whenever you succeed—and in the above case the teacher was manifestly right on the mark—you realize that it is the perfect recipe for what Steiner was keen on: what he called *economy in teaching*. Three minutes in that sense are about as economical as anything could be, though one should not exaggerate the time scale by ignoring the leading-in conversation and the subsequent song, poem or play or drawing—those aspects which have their own vibrancy and educational value, and which enable the 8-year-old to be *right in the middle of it*. On the one hand they enhance awareness of the all-important, never-to-be-retrod present moment—like a horny mountain peak that commands the prospect from every side—and on the other hand they allow the wisdom of the past to resonate so that it has a better chance of streaming forward in some form, though in all likelihood transformed into the eternal-seeking future.

And the consequences?

First and foremost, economy of teaching achieves interest—the opposite of having to sit through lessons in which the whole experience sits like lead in the soul (which in most cases might well be the fault of the pedagogical method the teacher is using to teach it). The adult has a similar feeling, perhaps, when the post delivers an envelope from a firm with whom one is having a long, sore-festering dispute. A lesson (or expression) which gives you the feeling of well-being is the opposite. You feel elated. Quite apart from the love of the child for the elator, there is the short-term preoccupation which it engenders, and the longer term interest, the longer term involvement of will to fathom the deeper significance of whatever it is.

In the case of fables, the knowledge of the story is arguably of limited merit. It is the moral implications that count, but this aspect of the story is conveyed through an image which, as with all images, can either be freely embraced by the listener or skimmed over. The morals that many editions of fables include as an appendage to the original narrative are the product of a later age (Victorian). The pictorial consciousness of an 8-year-old can only be lamed by such practices—and the will to consider what lives in the image of the fable is deadened by the subversive preaching that lurks in the damagingly added moral.

Where another topic is concerned, and one has one's sights on economy in teaching, the emphasis may be on beauty— the aesthetic beauty of a lyric poem or a piece of music. A third case might offer the child the opportunity of growing in their observational powers and their thinking—fathoming why, in trigonometry, the formula for *tangent* enables you to calculate the height of a building without having physically to get to the top, or putting oneself into Galileo's shoes in the cathedral at Pisa, watching the chandelier swinging and through inner effort discovering the law of the pendulum.

Thus true education becomes the means by which the child *grows*—psychologically, spiritually and in other ways. As the body develops, its physical dimension is triggered off by the release of hormones, the myelination of brain cells, and so on. At the other end of life it declines, by the disfunctioning of faculties, *sans teeth* etc. as Shakespeare put it so poignantly yet with touching humour. Education offers the teacher the possibility of adopting a midwife-like role in the birth of intelligence, faculties, skills and attitudes. Some of these may have more than useful outer consequences—coping with money, understanding an argument, caring for a budgerigar, etc.—and, with grace, may persist right into old age. All of them, without exception, have an effect on the unfolding character of the child. Three minutes spent telling a fable, if the circumstances are propitious—and Steiner gives good advice on how not simply to leave this to chance, but to get the children involved in such way that they are all ears when, at the end of the prelims, it is the teacher's turn to speak, at which she sets the jewel in the crown of the class's dialogue by telling the fable—three minutes can produce stimulation and enthusiasm in the soul, enlightenment and insight for the spirit, a feeling of well-being that pervades the body, and a little gem gladly received and highly valued in the treasure house of memory.

Layers of Consciousness

'What happens?'

I was on my way to the school office, a fairly heavy bag full of main-lesson books to be marked in one hand. There was not much time to change mental gear from the mythological vistas that had opened up—I had been telling Class 5 the latest episode of Prometheus—to the concentration needed for interviewing an applicant for the class. Steiner was keen that teachers keep honing their everyday skills such as planning school events, organizing meetings, preparing briefs for discussion, introducing and chairing faculty meetings, extending their sense of domestic economy to that of a complex 'business' such as a school, representing the client at formal meetings with professionals such as architects, being the public face of Waldorf on occasions such as a surgery with the local MP or a radio interview, and so on.

Take away these responsibilities from the teacher and there is the manifest danger that he would be lost in his ivory tower (e.g. the Prometheus saga, or some fine detail in projective geometry, or an absorbing point towards which his professional discipline had led him) and this, in turn, would subtly undermine the *pedagogical effectiveness* of his lessons. Of course, the complex finances of a school are usually too pivotal for the school's overall viability to risk leaving it in the hands of non-experts, so an adviser will certainly be needed if the administrator or bursar can't carry the burden of that responsibility on his own shoulders. And there is always the necessity of abiding by the law of any particular State and therefore to consider: what does it stipulate in such realms?

In such practical matters, Steiner was as innovative as in the cultural, spiritual realms. The bland argument *Take such responsibilities away from the teachers so that they are free to teach* was too short-sighted for him. Certainly give teachers whatever is possible to make them 'free' to teach (a look at their timetable and their remuneration might suggest areas that could well benefit from serious attention), but don't rob the children of effective lessons as a result of their teachers being excluded from being directly involved in the running of the school.

On this occasion it was an interview. With chalk-dust smudges brushed off my jacket, I was inwardly busy matching outer respectability (the school's face) and the inner receptivity that is necessary on such occasions. But I had not reckoned with what might happen as I crossed the playground to get from the classroom block to the school office complex where interviews took place.

With that uncanny knack that children can have of knowing when your guard is down, a bunch of four or five from Class 5 (aged 10/11) came bounding up and gleefully encircled me—*with intent*, although I didn't realize it until three minutes or so later! 'Imagine a twig from a hazel tree . . .' they began before I became aware that I was about to be led up the garden path (we had some hazel twigs in a vase in the classroom that were at that delicate early catkin stage which betokens the end of winter, even if overnight frosts still prevail and the occasional Arctic winds blast reminders that it's still only February). 'You bend the thin end into a loop and hold it in your left hand. Then with your right hand you pass the thicker end up through the loop *being careful that the two pieces don't touch* [an irrelevance, as I realized only later!]. Holding it in position, you revolve both hands at once, till the twig is facing the other way, and slowly, *slowly* lower the thick end into a bucket of water.' By this time my pictorial mind was completely riveted, as I was doing my utmost to imagine the situation, and follow the 'instructions' without letting the two ends of the twig (the looped and the thick) meet. So that when '*What happens?*' boomed out at me commandingly in chorus, I could do nothing but stare inwardly at the stalemate and the awkward, slightly contorted position that my hands and wrists had become somewhat locked in. The spokesperson at that point, having cleverly assessed how long the ensuing silence could be stretched out, and given a nod accordingly, was joined again by the ambushing revellers as they burst into my puzzlement with: '*It gets wet!*' They didn't hang about long after watching my face crease into laughter, before scurrying off in a cloud of triumphant merriment seeking their next victim.

What a lesson for the teacher who had just emerged from the imaginative vastness of the Prometheus myth, with its layers of possible interpretation, and who had then been enchanted into the image of a hazel twig to the point of near on mesmerization, and who needed to pull himself together so that at the forthcoming interview his unwritten checklist of questions would be systematically 'ticked'.

Moreover, it was essential that he should have been able to judge by the end of the interview (some 40 minutes later, maybe) where the consciousness of the potential newcomers to the class had got to. The family was Greek-Cypriot, with twins, a boy and a girl. With a matter as veiled and illusive as human consciousness in childhood, it's tricky discovering just what stage children have arrived at, even if their cultural background is familiar. I had never met a Greek-Cypriot before and was all agog wondering what bearing race, family, religion, climate, morphology, and other factors might have had on this crucial aspect of child development.

Attention has frequently been drawn to what could aptly be termed the three-tiered paradigm of Waldorf education. There are several aspects to this. Here we are looking at the consciousness that prevails in childhood. An air of *day-*

dreaminess is the norm into which the 10/11-year-old child easily subsides by default, with *imagery* being uppermost in the mind's awareness. Then follow years of transition (11/14) in which this state continues but exists alongside what is about to emerge as the eventual consciousness of adulthood itself: *rationality*. Rationality is a thought process that is ultimately as strong and neat as the strands that are spun together to produce a hank, say, of yarn from the best Cotswold wool. Some modes of thinking arrive at that neatness and strength almost instantaneously, like Athena born in full maturity from the forehead of Zeus. Other modes drift, or have to work hard to get there, going laboriously through all the mental processes equivalent to shearing the sheep, carding the fleece, and spinning the wool on the spinning wheel or distaff. Picture thinking on the other hand (the second stage in the three-tiered approach to consciousness) is of an essentially different nature. There it is not a matter of a single, unbroken thread of reason—a *linear* process. A picture is *two-dimensional*.

Prior to this, in the first stage of this three-tiered approach, is the Kindergarten child's consciousness, a consciousness that is at home in *space*. A spatial consciousness spills naturally into that space, into action, expresses itself through gesture, thrives and is stimulated by deeds being done and events materializing. In the presence of a pre-Waldorf-school child, the rational adult frequently needs to make an effort to forget that a chair is merely a dull chair. It can serve as a bus, a dentist's waiting room, a bed, a castle, a fishing boat, a bridge, anything that a spatial consciousness can 'see' in it, can conjure into it. Creative play again.

But to return to our starting point, from age 6/7–14 the inner picture prevails in consciousness, either complete like a fresco covering the entire wall of a refectory or a ceiling the size of the Sistine Chapel, or mosaic-like, flickering into the

mind as revealed in many children's drawings—with inter-
mediate stages, too. Wasn't Chagall an example of someone
who revisited that state of mind? But in his case, vibrant with
symbolism and with the artist's saturated feeling for colour,
there is much to suggest that he exercised more than one
layer of consciousness at a time.

The transition from picture-consciousness to reason at this
age requires careful handling. We would be the worse off if
we lost our ability to form mental representations. How
would we recognize one another? How would we appreciate
the beauty in, say, a Raphael cartoon? How would we come
to terms with what stared out at us from the mirror when we
brushed our hair each morning? What would we make of the
conventional sign warning the motorist to beware of deer
crossing the road, and a dozen and one other signs? What
would happen to the sense of majesty we experience in
recalling the colour-scape of a brilliantly sky-filled sunset?
Would we be able to enter the realm of the poet, whose key
to that realm lies so often in the images evoked?

Though these are hypothetical extremes, perhaps, they do
indicate that mental imagery plays a vital part in our lives.
More: neurological research would strongly suggest that it
plays an important part in the development of our rational
lives too, in that we are the worse off, apropos the func-
tioning of our left-brain hemisphere if the right hemisphere
has been neglected in childhood. Thus, education needs to
guard against vandalizing the 11-year-old's picture-
consciousness through focusing exclusively upon the emerging rational type of thinking evident at this age. Though
Steiner put this in different, certainly less confrontational
terms, he was emphatic about the importance of catering for
these distinct layers of consciousness throughout the curriculum and the pedagogy appropriate to teaching it.

To turn the harmless fun of the hazel loop getting wet into

an instructive parable, the teacher may greatly benefit from asking him/herself with regard to each topic taught and the methodology used: What is happening in the child's consciousness in the context of the three-tiered paradigm of Waldorf education?

The Teacher's Inner Life

'When were you there?'

It was in the mid 50s in one of the newly created Secondary Modern schools, where I was teaching part-time. It must have been one of the head teacher's first posts, for I remember him wearing his ermine hood, singing in the church choir during his Cambridge vacations a few years after 'the War'. In those days you could get a job teaching if you were qualified in the subject (as technically I was, both from my first honours degree and from my post-graduate work), though my qualified teacher status in today's sense was still two years away. Perhaps this went for others on the staff, if a remark made by the art teacher was anything to go by. He stopped me in the corridor one day—the only time I can recall his ever speaking to me!—and without any preamble or even a conventional greeting, commiserated: 'You and I are just here to take them when no one else wants them.'

I have to say, I couldn't tune into his pessimism and resolved week by week to inch a bit closer to those teenagers. I felt I was distinctly winning with the 11/13-year-olds but with the 14/16s tussled to find an effective way. Although it was a pre-Beatles era, there was plenty to distract youth from what would have then been termed 'good music'. So with the head's agreement I not only sang with the older classes but occasionally played them pieces which they were otherwise unlikely to care tuppence about.

The occasion in question—one which put new lenses into my pedagogical spectacles—was after a class had been listening to Mendelssohn's overture *Fingal's Cave*. I sometimes wonder whether any of those youngsters (who must now be on the verge of drawing their old age pensions) ever visited it with its great basaltic columns, towering supremely out of the turbulent ocean like huge ranks of organ pipes. At that point, the class was animated in a way I had not witnessed before. A group of pupils gathered round at the end of the lesson, wanting to know more. Some of the enthusiasm was for information: How do you get there? How long is the boat journey? Are the seas always rough? But it was the penetrating look from one pupil who asked, '*When were you there?*' that was the eye-opener for me. The question clearly came from an experience that had touched something deep within his soul, and I was fairly sure that it was not merely the slightly scratchy LP record that had done the trick. That 15-year-old had taken it for granted that what I had been describing, by way of introducing what they were about to hear, was from first-hand experience. In fact it was not. I hadn't at that time, and still never have, visited Fingal's Cave. Yet the atmosphere conveyed, and then more than confirmed by Mendelssohn's magnificent tone-portrayal, had obviously been one of *presence*—if that is the right word. Spiritual presence might be nearer the truth but I don't wish to convey anything spooky or, indeed, at all unreachable by that.

Spiritual presence is not charisma. The latter tends to achieve permanence and is personal—something that can almost be felt when you read the name of the charismatic 'star' in the Radio Times. You would not expect a class to feel sentiment of that kind about a Hebridean island—certainly not teenagers. There are too many ups and downs, for one thing, even in the course of a 40-minute lesson. But it is reasonable to expect (even despite the downs) that one of the lesson's trajectories might reach the height of this 'presence'—at least for the pupils. The teacher—especially if he is over-melancholic—may reflect on the learning curve that the downs are telling him about. But where there is a sense of presence, even if it is only momentary, education, I believe, is taking place.

I was emphatically reminded of this when visiting a Waldorf school in Israel. The education in the country as a whole had only been established for some six years. The equivalent stage in England would take us back to 1932! So experience was only very slowly gathering momentum and moving towards its first affirmations. The 'lead' teacher taking Class 1 had been trained in Switzerland and had done teaching practice in Germany. He realized that his experience there was light-years away from the Middle East with its ethnic mix, with its distinctly Asiatic nuance, with its (for Germany) unheard of informality and with Israel's unequivocal adherence to another religious tradition (even to some extent for non-believers). Therefore he was ultra-sensitive to what should be given emphasis in the sense of *Jewish* Waldorf, on the one hand, and what, on the other hand, in his view should be regarded as too Eurocentric to have relevance for Israel, and so should either be dropped or only be given tangential reference. And that was even before the present political confrontations that have raged there so tragically around the Palestinian question.

Class 3, as we have already seen, includes a study of the Old Testament, the most significant of all Hebrew literature. Where could you feel more at home in this corner of the Waldorf curriculum than in Israel? So with this bit firmly between his Israeli teeth, he confidently cantered through the Class 4 curriculum, *shedding* the Norse mythology that had become such a tradition in other parts of the world—a very popular and usually much-loved tradition amongst pupils, it should be stressed. Not that his class suffered through this: I personally taught them years later in Class 12 for a main-lesson block and they were exemplary Waldorf pupils, without any shadow of a doubt. When, however, the next

Class 4 came along, their class teacher was not convinced that her colleague's decision to drop Norse mythology would be right for her group. Suppressing all doubt about whether it would look too Germanic to a wary parental body, and overcoming the slight flutter of trepidation that she felt at her colleague's quizzical frowns when he heard about her intentions, she launched into the topic with a determined will, preparing the ground by plunging into the sea-roving life of the Vikings, the last adherents to Odin, Thor, Freja, Loki and the other dwellers in Asgard. (After all, don't we still feel some weekly kinship somewhere, via Tiewsday, Odinsday, Thorsday, Frejasday?)

The main-lesson had hardly been going many days when she reported to an astonished faculty a remark that one of her pupils had made after her morning's efforts. 'Please Miss, were *you* once a Viking?' I don't suppose she had time to answer the question in the maelstrom of the main-lesson, but who knows?

Are such responses elicited from the children by the teacher shaking the substance of the lesson out of her sleeve? Undoubtedly sometimes there are those unforgettable moments in the teaching day when something seems to come to your aid, moments to be profoundly grateful for. Perhaps, just as the Tibetan seer traditionally possesses a 'third eye', the teacher develops a third sleeve! But in the main, it isn't enough to rely on that. Teaching is a profession and professions have their discipline. The professional meditative material that is amongst the legacy that Steiner left for the Waldorf Movement, if worked assiduously and with integrity, enables the teacher to begin to plumb the depths of his or her own being. It is from such depths that enlivening powers of description well. The teacher comes closer to the material than mere abstract knowledge permits, however important it is also to be factually correct. The dry bones of knowledge—be it knowledge of Fingal's Cave, Norse mythology, atomic theory, permutations and combinations, tectonic plates, or any topic that crops up in class—need fleshing out if the learning is going to be a healthy experience, of developmental relevance, and something whose currency lasts in some form or other throughout life.

The response of the Israeli class to the Norse mythology main-lesson ensured its place for subsequent classes. It is quite possible, however, that the response would not have carried sufficient weight if, in her inner life, the teacher had made no attempt to be spiritually present, *to be there*. There's something like a motto to be unveiled here: the teacher's inner, meditative life engenders the kind of spiritual presence that enables her to lift the class, as if on the back of a winged Pegasus, into hitherto unexplored realms.

Grammar: Through the Gateway of Thinking to Discovering the World

'Nevertheless.'

I was conducting a seminar on the teaching of the grammar of the mother tongue. It was in Northern Ireland where, somewhat unexpectedly, the seminarists were a particularly international bunch. This meant that I had to rely on a good deal of inner translation going on. My problem, however, was not one of getting the meaning across; it was having to refer to something that can *only* be experienced in the mother tongue. Even if you are happy thinking in English, if you have not grown up in the language it will be impossible to recall what it was like for you when, sometime during childhood, you began to realize for the first time the significance of a particular part of speech. This might be the latest fashion in adolescent interjections, or a tense whose dimensions opened up a new vista of perception (such as the future perfect), or even the grammatical power and stylistic elegance of the semicolon. When we speak a language other than our mother tongue, apart from a few unusual offerings gathered from the cornucopia of life, we are likely to be inclined to remain where we feel safest: among basics—the most common irregular verbs, pleasantries so that we can get along in our social life, clichés for finding our way around town, an idiom or two, fairly pedestrian vocabulary, a very limited choice of roll-off-the-tongue interjections, and probably little else. In that Northern Irish seminar, however, we had time and opportunity for interaction (unlike a formal lecture), so it slowly became possible for everyone to dig deep into their mother tongue memories.

On the occasion I have in mind I had reached Class 6 (age 12) and its age-related part of speech, first reviewing the sequence of preposition (Class 4 emphasis) and conjunction (Class 5 emphasis). A student from Middle Europe sat there beaming with obvious pleasure. She had been thinking about the whole stream of grammar teaching, and at the mention of 'conjunction' the beam became wider and her complexion rosier. I paused with raised eyebrows, sensing she had something to say. She did. Like a length of red carpet being unrolled outside a hotel entrance for a VIP's arrival, out it came, one single word, her latest acquisition in English as a foreign language: '*Nevertheless!*' With aplomb, she waited until the entire length of carpet had unrolled so that the rest of us could walk on it, so to speak, and gain access to its unusual sound, its rhythm, its meaning, its grammatical potential—its conjunctional prowess.

Perhaps it is slightly cheating to cite an adult foreign national's reaction to English grammar, but the incident not only has charm, it makes 'visible' (not because of memory, but because of the adult consciousness which could express in clear thoughts the process going on) the inner awakening which is particularly goaded by grammar teaching à la Waldorf, and which is going on a good deal less visibly in children of the age we are considering. The same can be said for younger children, too, since grammar teaching begins no later than Class 2 or 3. The heightening of self-awareness in the children's own mental processes, however, is a vital factor in their development at this crucial stage of 11+ and it is nurtured at several levels. In grammar of the mother tongue, *memory* and *thinking* are called into play in tandem; in the Waldorf phenomenological approach to science, the awakening thinking is approached via the *senses*.

First, let us briefly remind ourselves of the journey that leads to this point. Lessons in *natural science* have been preceded by three preparatory stages: (i) the continuously changing seasonal *experience* of nature in Kindergarten (and incidentally of natural laws—when walking over a bridge, riding on a rocking horse, blowing a dandelion 'clock', and so on); (ii) the nature *story* at the outset of the Lower School, which directs the child's attention in two opposite but complementary ways, towards a phenomenological detail that is unfolding in nature, and towards the 'atmosphere' attaching to the natural object of which the detail is a part; and (iii) the three kingdoms of nature of animal, plant and mineral, in Classes 4, 5 and 6 respectively (*natural history*, so-called), each related to some aspect of the human being. The thread in common is the concentration, at one level of consciousness or another, upon the phenomena that nature presents. In very broad terms, at first it is at an *experiential* level, secondly predominantly at a *feeling* level, and thirdly purely *observational*. Finally, at age 12 and in all the classes thereafter, an *understanding* for what is observed is cultivated through the following procedure.

The phenomena are first presented by the teacher. The children need to know *what* it is they are looking at (or touching, or listening to, etc.) but it is essential to the procedure that no explanation as to *why* things behave or react or appear as they do is as yet given. At age 12 such presentations will include—maybe predominate in—phenomena that are part of the children's life experience: colours of clouds in the sky, different sounds made by wind or waterfall, the varied resonances of different timbers, the behaviour of common materials in heat or cold, the changing appearance of a landscape at the first glimmer of dawn, and so on. From such 'natural' occurrences, which are considered in the various branches of physics (acoustics, light, colour, heat, etc.), phenomena are presented for which some laboratory equipment is required, the latter increasing in complexity year by year as the study of each branch progresses.

After this presentation, the teacher is then required to step aside from the apparatus—or cease referring directly to the natural phenomenon if that is what the children's attention has been drawn to—and briefly but incisively create for the children what is essentially a *pictorial metaphor* of the phenomenon under consideration. I hesitate to use the word 'fantasy', as this is open to misinterpretation. Neither shall I relay the example to which Steiner himself refers at this point, which can easily be looked up by those wishing to go more deeply into the matter.

Only the *next* day, after sleep has intervened, and after the phenomenon has been recalled by the class, are the children asked to *think* about what has been observed, the thinking thus arriving at the 'law' by which the phenomenon can be *understood*.

For those familiar with Goethe's scientific work, the foregoing procedure will be reminiscent of his phenomenological approach. It is essentially the fourth step in the children's scientific schooling (experience, feeling, observation, understanding) concentrating particularly on leading sense observation into thinking-understanding, into rationality.

If grammatical laws give us an insight into the structure of language—and the list would indeed be lengthy if one aggregated *all* the laws in *all* languages spoken on the face of the earth!—would it be pressing a point too far to suggest that schooling the senses to observe a phenomenon, and the thinking to truly understand it, is tantamount to gaining access to the language of the Creative Logos? For example, 'Let there be Light!' incorporates one grammatical Logos-law; while 'Let us make "Man" in our own image' incorporates another. Apologies for what I realize is cumbersome

language. I am not in the slightest wanting to coin terminology—I am only attempting to introduce an idea. The
Logos grammatical structures of rainbows, natural cupolas as in
caves, clouds at sunset, eddies at the water's edge, dandelions
shooting up through tarmac, salt crystals, rhodochrosite,
alcohol, metal fatigue, yawning—how would the Logos have
phrased, 'Let there be yawning'?—elephants' graveyards,
Siamese twins, migrating birds, hippopotami (them again!),
olive oil, 'eye of newt', eyelashes of reindeer, cancer cells,
Jupiter's moons, earth tremors, the right hemisphere of the
brain, club feet, and a million other phenomena, must all
eventually be discoverable.

The list would seem endless. *Nevertheless,* human observation combined with enhanced thinking must surely be able
to summon and develop the capacities required to get there
in the end.

Authority and Creative Discipline

'See you at gardening.'

The circumstances were not typically Waldorf. In the class of mainly 12-year-olds were a few younger children, the school's intention being to open a new class for one of the groups as soon as numbers of applicants warranted it. The Waldorf maxim of teaching a subject at a particular age with an appropriate methodology to gain optimum educational benefit is, of course, totally incompatible with the so-called combined class (though a combined Waldorf class might still be preferable for some parents to other forms of education available to them). In these circumstances, the children were going out to break after main-lesson, changing into their outdoor clothes.

The school had employed a very good gardening teacher who nevertheless was finding this particular group a handful during the first few weeks of term, so I, as class teacher, accompanied them to the lesson whenever I could. Due to a prior engagement one week I had been unable to do this and the resultant tension, caused through the gardening teacher's authority not quite having established itself, had been too much for the youngest member of the class. When, therefore, the week after, I remarked as they were changing into their wellies, 'See you at gardening,' his relief, much to everyone's astonishment, came out forcibly as: *'Thank God!'*

It comes as something of a surprise that Steiner set so much store on *authority*. Especially is this so as it is unfashionable in an age which appeals so much to the young child's *reason* rather than simply stating, when your child at the supermarket checkout questions your refusal to buy some enticingly packaged junk food, 'Because I say so.'

The concept of the Waldorf class teacher, someone who remains with the class for ages 6–14 and teaches the subjects that require less knowledge or skills from the teacher, i.e. *not* foreign languages, music (orchestral ensembles and choir), gymnastics, eurythmy, handwork or woodwork (religion is a case on its own), is based on the principle of authority. This is a stage beyond the Kindergarten. There the adult is the one who embodies the principle of *imitation*. The soul-spirit of the child is incarnating into the body. Even the mammal-like use of the body entails the power of imitation, but beyond this, that which raises human beings above their mammal-like nature is also frequently 'embodied' in imitative activity.

At age 7–14, it is not that the power of imitation is no longer accessible to the child; even as adults we continue to rely on this for some things (try learning or teaching the meticulously placed foot movements of a Scottish Highland sword dance *without* imitation if you want to convince yourself of this!). But there is a shift of emphasis. The rapport between the learning child and the adult moves inwards, from being bodily based to soul-prompted. Though still at a dreamlike level, the soul of the child is awaking. But the awaking is sufficient for the child to seek a more inward connection with the adult world. The child's teachers before birth, one could say, were of a divine order. Now the child looks for what is worthy of emulation in the adult world and, finding that, experiences inner growth and development in the presence of the adult, the one who has 'gone before'. This comes to particular expression through *language*. The language spoken by the teacher carries not only factual meaning, but also expresses soul nuances. In that experience, hearing human language, the child's soul 'breathes' and, just as fresh mountain air endows the body with health and strength, so the linguistic air which the child breathes—providing it is imbued with the right qualities—induces a feeling of well-being, of growth for the soul.

What are those right qualities?

In answer to this question, it is perhaps helpful to couple the concept of authority with that of *discipline*. Discipline problems invariably occur where authority has broken down. Though it is perhaps slightly stretching a point, the two words can be connected linguistically: discipline via *disciple* and authority via *author*. He or she who experiences inner growth and who gladly acknowledges the one who is 'author' of it—would *co-author* be nearer the truth?—becomes the disciple of that author/co-author. What is here evident at a linguistic level can easily be translated into terms that apply to the classroom or to the home.

But this still does not answer the question: What are the *qualities* 7/14-year-olds perceive as the 'voice of authority', to the extent that they freely accord the speaker authoritative status? For Steiner, the answer lay in the realm of the arts. Of course, an increase in knowledge represents a certain degree of growth. But even if we downloaded all the knowledge on the internet, say, and committed it to memory, it is highly questionable whether that would constitute an *artistic* experience. Similarly it is with skills. Although we feel empowered by the ability to multiply, to throw a javelin, to conjugate a verb in Russian, to put the correct fingers down on the correct cello string to produce a certain note in tune, to get into our email, to knit a sock, to prune a rose-bush or to make a mortise and tenon joint, we can do no more than *apply* the skill(s) we have learnt when needed. We draw on knowledge; we apply skills. With the arts, however, we become *creative*. Whether it be the art of telling a story well, of playing a Haydn minuet beautifully, of decorating a birthday cake tastefully, of using our watercolours harmoniously, of expressing in clay the calm mood of a ruminating cow, of moving a piece of eurythmic choreography gracefully, or simply shaping the letters of the essay we are writing pleasingly, whatever artistic activity we are engaged in expands the soul, brings another dimension beyond the confines of citing knowledge or applying a skill—a *creative* dimension.

When the teacher cultivates an artistic way of storytelling, of handling the recorder, of writing on the chalk board, of formulating her sentences, of transforming the presentation of bare facts through an imaginative pedagogy and so on, she creates an ethos in the classroom in which the children experience how they 'breathe' more healthily at a soul level. Through this, when they go on to those parts of the lesson in which they themselves are active participators, they continue to move, think or feel within the artistically creative ethos which prevails. The teacher, one could say, has authored the growth that ensues. This results in discipline which is the wholehearted outcome of authorship rather than grudgingly conceded within the confines of authoritarianism.

When Steiner speaks of children loving their teachers (a phrase—even a concept—which sits more comfortably, perhaps, on German-speaking shoulders than English), he is not meaning anything that is remotely namby-pamby. It is a quality of heart, pure in essence and free from sentimentality. Conversely, he emphasized that education today cannot depend on the teacher simply loving the child. This is not to deny that such an approach was sufficient in the distant past. Today, however, the attitude towards the child's present and future development needs to be advanced professionally into a continuously practised *art* of pedagogy. At first hearing, it can come as a mild shock that love for the child doesn't go far enough. But it makes sense when one realizes that it is a matter of how to express the love. A 'difficult' child, particularly, will often reveal how far we have managed to get.

The teacher's love for the child allied to his or her inner work will both inform lesson preparation and evoke spontaneity at the chalkface. It will soon come across as the right *how* and will engender in the years we are concerned with the feeling of true authority. The children will thus reciprocate with a *creatively disciplined* response. It will be a far cry from the discipline of the parade ground or the prison cell—a rigid type discipline that is marked by the children sitting bolt upright at their desks etc. But equally it will not deteriorate into the sloppy kind of discipline that results from over-familiarity, or laxity in lesson preparation, or ambition on behalf of the teacher, or self-indulgence, or any of the other undesirables that sooner or later deteriorate or miss the mark. An ideal? Certainly, but one in which, even if one doesn't fully attain it in each and every lesson (we are only human, after all), the children will blossom.

Even though the fast-becoming-fashionable term *kindergarden* sounds like a strange and unnecessary linguistic jumble to some ears, at least it brings home how similar in some respects teaching and gardening are. It certainly behoves the teacher to practise her creative discipline—weeding, pruning, hoeing, staking, watering, earthing up, mulching, transplanting, grafting, harvesting, dead-heading, not to overlook *admiring* as and when necessary. The teacher could do well to ponder the metaphor—though it is not by any means the first time it has been used. It is even reminiscent of the scene in which Shakespeare takes us into the palace garden at Kings Langley in *Richard II*—a timely warning to the dissolute king, which alas went unheeded.

The above attempts to elaborate Steiner's view that creative discipline was entirely connected with the arts in the middle years 7–14. He or she who assiduously cultivates the arts, and above all the art of anthroposophically imbued pedagogy, will discover *their* way of authority. Society has demanded that corporal punishment be superseded in disciplinary matters. Perhaps it will eventually arrive at eliminating 'soul punishment' too. This does not necessitate more 'rules' in the book. The genuine way is through inner work, and where such a teacher is present and active in the garden of education one might well add: 'Thank God!'

Cultivating an Evolutionary Attitude

'When will the present epoch end?'

Her seriousness and adult-like intensity of gaze when she posed the question surprised me. It was an astronomy main-lesson in Class 7. In pursuing the phenomenological approach, I was introducing the class to the concept of the *precession of the equinoxes* which is connected with how the sun can be observed to rise each year at the vernal equinox in relation to the zodiac. Taking the constellations as an average, each twelfth of the zodiac is traversed by the sun during a period of 2160 years. Without going into what would be termed astrology, it is therefore possible to link each 2160-year period with its corresponding part of the zodiac which, of course, forms a circle behind the sun's apparent path in the sky, the ecliptic.

A hand shot up during all those fairly complex, time-consuming concepts—certainly mind-stretching for 13-year-olds, which, within limits, is a good thing. Not being able to immediately roll the answer off the tip of my tongue, I went to the board, wrote down the date in the fifteenth century at which the present epoch is said to have begun, added 2160 to it and underlined the answer. With a very determined gesture, the obviously awakened young questioner inclined her somewhat unkempt mop of curls, stabbed at her notebook with her pencil and wrote down the answer—it was difficult to gauge whether it was with satisfaction at knowing just where she stood in the panorama of evolution. Perhaps it had been with annoyance that so much time had slipped by with so little achieved thus far by what she frustratingly perceived was a lethargic humanity. Or was it with the added spur she needed to roll up her sleeves and change the world, the choleric reaction to life which murmurs or seethes in the minds of most adolescents at some stage in their development, that stage usually spilling well over into the twenties.

Class 7 (rising 13) is a vital turning point towards the end of the second seven-year period of childhood. The personality begins to blossom in a new way. Thoughts, feelings and actions become more and more *personalized*. Not, perhaps, the steady well-balanced personalization of the adult—there are far too many half-formed opinions and flaring or moody emotional outbursts for that as a rule. Yet the veil of childhood is peeled off and, beneath, the *person* who is going to become the chalice for the incoming ego is revealed— coming out, as it were, like stars at night spread sparingly but with infinite beauty right across the vault of heaven. The sunniness of childhood, albeit with its weepy clouds and unexpected squalls, changes into a night sky of bright planets, hardly discernible distant stars, clear constellations, the occasional comet, and a Milky Way of ever-adventurous soul enquiry, discovery and daring. Small wonder Steiner adopted the old Persian word for the member of the human being that comes to the fore at this age (the third septennial phase, 14– 21): the *astral* organization.

The whole process is one of inner awakening: awakening to the power of thought increasingly at one's command, awakening to the shades, nuances, range and pressures of the emotional life, awakening to what needs to flow strongly into the realm of resolve which becomes the spring of our actions. Steiner catered admirably for the advent of all this by the inclusion of the main-lesson already referred to as 'Wish, Wonder and Surprise'. *Wishing* comes in a whole pageant of different costumes; it is there in covetousness, yearning, prayer, envy, altruism, fantasy, benediction, curse, not to mention commonplaces such as rummaging at the January sales! Likewise there is a whole spectrum of experiences associated with *wonder* and *surprise*, though the soul-gesture of all three is very different. The main-lesson block aims to make the pupils aware of these soul-gestures, their degree of intensity, their light or dark, their positive or negative attributes, and from that awareness to cultivate a more and more refined *ability to express in language* what has personally been experienced. This could be described as Waldorf creative writing *par excellence*.

With such new-found inner awareness, consolidated by the ability to fashion words in such a way that they convey the power of thought and feeling in the inner life, the pupils are ready to gain the richness of 'travelling' through lands across the globe, far beyond the confines of the continent in which they live. They can also explore those tendencies and movements in history—the Renaissance, the Reformation and the Age of Discovery—which were the currents surging in the great turning of the tide between those states of consciousness which prevailed in the Old World and the New.

The impressions of childhood very often remain subconscious; they are woven into the whole fabric of our being. As we grow older, however, while impressionable experiences still continue to become part of the woven whole, more and more of them stand out from the fabric of life, even as a thicker twine stands out 'proud' upon the weft's undershot.

The other main-lessons that frequently form part of the Waldorf curriculum at this age, mechanics and human biology (from the point of view of health, hygiene and nutrition), form a polarity in this respect. Mechanics presents some of the basic principles found in the physical world (the inclined plane, the lever, the pulley etc.); human biology energizes a deeper enquiry than has taken place in earlier years into the complexity, the wonder and, yes, the mystery of the human organism.

While we can put a date to the end of the present epoch, it is an awe-inspiring thought that we can by no means assign a date to that point at which we shall fully understand such human mysteries. This fact drives and nourishes the adolescent's idealism, if it is to be healthily grounded and not fantastical or removed and remote from the reality of life.

So while the sun and stars define when our present epoch shall give over to the next, we need to 'count our lucky stars' and be grateful to them for what we have personally received—something that one cannot expect the adolescent overtly to be terribly fussy about, needless to say. At the same time, we need to be proactive in placing in the 'azure vault' of evolution stars of idealism by which we can steer our course of life in a self-determined way, so that when the present epoch does end at least some of the squibs in the firework display which will celebrate the occasion will not be too damp to ignite. This the adolescent can readily identify with. And woe betide the educationist who fails to recognize the fact—and its practical implications for the next generation—inadvertently or otherwise and irrespective of whether his thumb be in the political, the chalk-facial or the parental slice of the educational pie!

The Incoming Ego and the Watershed of Adolescence

'I know her by her gait.'

Shakespeare scholars will wonder why I am quoting a line from *The Tempest*. It was in 1966, the first Class 8 play I had put on. I was full of admiration for how the class had worked in rehearsals, borne as much by class spirit and an inherent enthusiasm as by their teacher and the force of circumstances. Now we were showing the fruits of our efforts to the parents, friends and teachers at the farewell party, where class and class teacher take leave of one another—they to continue into the Upper School with specialists for each subject, their teacher (at least in those days, a standard occurrence), to retrace his or her way 'back' to Class 1, to begin the eight-year journey all over again.

I had conducted rehearsals from the auditorium, naturally. On this occasion, however, I was prompting the scene from the wings—the masque which the betrothed Miranda and Ferdinand witness in Act IV. Imagine my astonishment when the Goddess Juno—whose cue to go on stage was that very line: 'Great Juno comes; I know her by her gait,'—a tall girl in the class, chosen for her commanding presence, was suddenly shoved onto the stage in a remarkable, ungoddesslike way by two of her peers. She said her lines, showing little evidence of the stage fright of which her friends evidently had foreknowledge, and then, at the earliest permissible moment, melted with a sigh into the welcomingly safe anonymity of the folds of the blue curtains which comprised the wings. Her expression as soon as she was offstage was a strange cocktail of triumph and relief, with a slight touch of mischief (the cherry in the cocktail?) at the ruse she'd connived at crossing the threshold from being incognito in the wings to entering the glare of the footlights—by eliciting the help of a couple of adolescents who were as determined as she was that their show would proceed without a blemish.

Presumably anyone can be overcome with stage fright. But this wasn't *anyone*—it was a girl on the cusp of passing from the second to the third seven years. Steiner speaks in terms of *birth* in relation to this new phase of development. A less imaginative way of putting it would be 'the emancipation of the astral nature from the inherited organism of etheric-physical'. One meets plenty of people who, when that emancipation reaches a point of climax—around age 18 is not unusual—leave the family home and strike out on their own. Going to university might be seen as a more formal version of the same thing. There is, of course, more at stake; for the decision to take the fairly drastic step of going it alone *for the first time in life* is a step taken not as the result of the inexorable turning of the academic wheel but by the incoming individuality. But this in turn is rooted (it could be pictured as the main taproot) in the astral. In either case, the individuality, which is unique and the most independent member of our human makeup, is embedded in the becoming-emancipated astral, and together they set sail from the harbour of childhood (the family home often being the external manifestation of this) out into the ocean of life.

If there is sense in Steiner's use of the concept of 'birth' to describe this stage of emancipation, then we would expect to see indications of something that is tender, new, apprehensive, maybe. The incident cited in the Class 8 play is a good example. A pupil whose work was 'top notch', who certainly had more than a touch of the melancholic's meticulousness and who, looked at with that Janus face which specializes in hindsight, through the previous childhood years, was a fully mature 14-year-old, now experienced despite this maturity the birth of a deep part of her nature. And she was temporarily thrown. Those temporary moments of bashfulness happen to most of us at that adolescent stage, notwithstanding a plethora of other occasions when we doorslammed, were defiant in our disobedience, strutted like a cock on the dunghill, expressed outlandish opinions, followed with apparent impunity the erring crowd...

For the educationist, therefore, in Class 8 there is a (last) opportunity to bring what is needed for this birth and for the often long gestation period that leads up to it. A rich array of subjects comes to the teacher's aid: dressmaking in handwork; the three-dimensional construction of the five Platonic solids in geometry; the encounter with the skeleton in human biology; the first in-depth study of poetry in literature; the addition of meteorology to the other sciences that are taught at this age (meteorology whose keynote is changeability, an outer reflection of the very element sparked off by the inner changes occurring at this time already referred to); emphasis on the global ecological problems we create for ourselves and our descendants and approaches towards their solution in geography; and the seething spirit of social upheaval played out through various revolutions in history (Industrial, French, American, Risorgimento, Bolshevik, etc.), all crammed into the last four hundred years. And without labouring, but nonetheless not losing sight of the point, *drama*.

When Rudolf Steiner was invited to be amongst the guests of honour at the conference for New Ideals in Education, held in Stratford-upon-Avon in 1922 shortly after the First World War, he stressed that in education there could be no drama before adolescence. What was he driving at? And where does it leave all the class plays that are such an integral part of Waldorf school life from age 7–13?

To answer the first question, we need go no further than

look once more at the difference between the astral and the etheric. As we have seen, the astral nature of the child is the very force—*being* would not be too strong a way of putting it—behind the mask of adolescence. Though absolutely vital in our lives, its effect on the physical body needs cushioning. This task, which falls to the etheric, is carried out successfully if the health of the etheric 'body' has been nurtured in childhood without undue interference. In modern life—and the more urbanized it is, the more is this the case—such interference is unavoidable. The ceaseless, 24-hours-per-day noise of traffic and other machinery interposing itself between the child and nature—let alone something like the bludgeoning siren, say, of a fire engine—is, perhaps, the most widespread example. It therefore behoves the adult carers of children (partners, teachers, hostel wardens, etc.) to provide extra protection and nurturing for the etheric from birth onwards in all the pre-adolescent years. Such protection constitutes, amongst other things, preparation for modern life, a fact which the attitude of 'throw them in at the deep end so they'll get used to it' clearly does not take into account. Thus as far as is practicable the child is protected from the drama of modern life evident in the bombardment of the senses (not only through noise), the rush and tension, the obliteration of so much of the natural world, etc.—until the member which can take it (the astral) begins to develop the strength of independence in adolescence, a strength which will help it to become a fit vessel for the ever-incarnating ego.

In the *class play*, a new one as like as not, practised and performed usually once in a year, the teacher possesses a powerful means for that very task of nurturing the etheric. The *language*, especially in the first five classes of the Lower School, can be entirely rhythmical; the *structure* of the play can enhance the imagery connected with the narrative from which the 'plot' of the play has been drawn; the *gestures*, the *movement* of the characters, the *tableaux* built up on stage can all further kindle the images that reside in the child's memory as a result of that narrative. When Waldorf educationists speak of the role of art being to *deepen* the child's experience of the subject, the more regular, day-by-day ways of doing this are mainly through artistic conversational recall, creative writing, modelling, singing, painting, drawing or the improvisatory acting or miming of a situation. But although a formal play lasting between 10 and 30 minutes does not fall into this category of daily usage, it nevertheless deepens the child's experience of the subject matter, precisely *because* it takes so long to rehearse and bring off (between four and six weeks is favourable). That is to say, the play helps the intake of the subject healthily to 'arrive' at the etheric nature of the child. Later, when the wish to *understand* is transformed by the astral dawning from dreamy first light to the radiant colours of sunrise, the pictorial richness resting in the etheric is there, ready to be drawn on like water from a full reservoir. Still later, when the adult's astrality thirsts for knowledge and understanding, directing its attention back to one of those Lower School play topics in which macrocosmic imagin-ations have been 'recorded', implanted in narrative by our forefathers (The Golden Goose, David and Goliath, Thor's Hammer, Perseus slaying the Medusa before rescuing Andromeda from the jaws of the serpent), hopefully the adult ego will be there to shove the striving astral from where it stands in ignorance in the dark wings of abstraction onto the stage of the etheric, where insight is to be found and where the ego will be able to recognize *the dawning truth*.

Form, Freedom and Fantasy

'Windsor Castle on washing day!'

Another Class 8 play! The incident in question occurred some months before the performances were scheduled. Preparation was well underway. Even before I had decided which play would suit the class, I had by good fortune discovered a theatre in North London which put on productions in as near Shakespeare's original style as possible. At least the stage area emulated the original Globe Theatre. There I attended a hilarious performance of one of the comedies and an impressive *Richard II*. It was the production side of the latter that had commanded my attention. The bare wooden stage became a riot of colour each time someone came on the scene who bore a coat of arms. A retainer in livery came on with the character and stood in the background holding high banner or flag, according to what the occasion demanded—the interior of a noble court or the clamour and clang of the field of battle.

From that experience, my mind leapt rapidly to *Henry V* and I immediately started researching the heraldry of the time. Though I unearthed some detail from standard encyclopaedias, the picture was not complete, and I drew inexplicably disappointing blanks concerning those characters who appear in the play who hailed from the French side of the Channel. So I phoned the College of Heraldry in London where someone with a courteously cooperative and very cultivated voice answered. But imagine my amusement (and part despair) when, at my request, 'Please could you tell me how to locate the heraldry for the French nobility who fought at the Battle of Agincourt at the beginning of the fifteenth century?' there was first a thick silence, followed by a forlorn, slightly posh but cockney-laced accent oozing through the receiver: 'Er . . . I don't think we could 'elp yer 'ere Sir!'

My next move was to go second-hand book shop scouring. Apart from a few unsuccessful sallies locally, I set my sights on Charing Cross Road, London, one of the most concentrated such areas I could think of within reasonable reach. Starting at the southern end, I found nothing remotely helpful. Thinking I was looking for a specialist volume, I had somehow discounted the big stores—in fact I was not even aware that the mammoth Foyles had a second-hand department. After a weary couple of hours traipsing from shop to shop, coming out empty-handed each time and feeling somewhat disconsolate, I stood on the pavement and somehow dragged myself by default—the only way I can describe it—onto a red London double-decker bus. The buses were all open where you alighted in those days with perky conductors collecting fares and overseeing public safety, etc. The one in command on the bus I boarded commented, when a nimble 50-year-old hopped onto the vehicle as it was pulling away from some traffic lights: 'Been to Lourdes have we!?'

As I got off (wondering whether a visit to Lourdes might not, in fact, be the very thing I needed to lift my spirits!) I saw Foyles second-hand book department right next to the bus stop. Surprised and cautiously pleased, I hastened my step and within what seemed like seconds had walked to the very shelf and there spotted the very reference work I sorely needed: *Shakespeare's Heraldry.*

From that moment, the momentum gathered immense pace. Within days, I had encouraged the class to beg for old sheets which we dyed for the background colours of our banners etc. We made templates for fleurs-de-lis and for lions both rampant and couchant, etc. Using emulsion paint, we transformed the threadbare, throw-away lengths of cotton sheet into livery to wear and banners to wave ostentatiously to the beat of drum, or droop in docile silence in the background, according to the mood of each scene.

It was on one of these costume and prop making occasions that a bright spark in the class began running out of patience—perfectly understandable, even if she hadn't been an ambitious adolescent—in meticulously painting her umpteenth rampant lion's claw(!) and brought the house down with : 'Mr Masters, can't we just put ditto marks?' And on another when, having been out to the loo, the 'Earl of Warwick' breezed back into the classroom—which by now was adorned with clothes lines we'd rigged up on which semi-completed costumes were draped and 'Wet paint, work-in-progress' was hanging up to dry. Surveying all this, the Earl (a blacksmith's son who could be quite taciturn) sparkled, 'Hmm—looks like Windsor Castle on washing day in here!'

This illustrates two vital pedagogical points. *Yes*, the young people are entering their final seven-year phase of childhood at age 14 when the soul's thought powers will be in the ascendancy. *No*, this is definitely not the time to neglect the other attributes of the soul—the powers of will and the strong currents of feeling. In the above context, Shakespeare's cut and thrust more than adequately caters for the latter, but at the same time engages the will, so that the young person can fully identify with whatever activity is requiring a modicum of skill, bearing in mind that today there is no lack of surrogate will 'activities' in whose web the unwary teenager can easily get caught up.

The other pedagogical point seriously to bear in mind is that we do the awakening thinking of the adolescent a severe disservice if we only feed it with rationality. Of course, causal thinking is the very stuffing of so much that goes on in our lives. We cannot make headway without its clarity and sharp-edgedness, nor without the unbroken thread which it can provide in the dark mazes in which we may find ourselves—often face to face with one Minotaur or another. On the Lower School side of the wide threshold of adolescence—and Class 8 is still at that juncture—teachers will do well to provide for this growing need by engaging the pupils in such mathematical disciplines as simultaneous equations in algebra (the introduction to powers also enables a start on quadratics to be made), the application of all kinds of formulae, a wide variety of problems in three-dimensional geometry, the ebb and flow of money in a multitude of realms (purchase, investment, donation, tax, water rates, insurance, pensions, mortgage, hire purchase, capital gains), and so on. This is in addition to the phenomenological approach to science as described earlier.

The thinking must also be given room for 'play', however, as demonstrated by the above comments. When Steiner exhorted the teachers to teach grammar *with humour*, he was already setting up a prominent signpost pointing in this direction. But play does not simply end with fun. *Creativity* in thinking can be applied to all three realms of soul. The inventor directs it towards outer substance. The artist uses material (watercolour, clay, ballet shoes, trombones, laser printers, reinforced concrete, and so on) to convert and communicate what he or she experiences as creative thought/feeling. Fun too: the jester's creative thinking goes tantalizingly pitter-pat on the tin roof of the mind and 'sets the table on a roar' as Hamlet so nostalgically put it, when recalling his beloved Yorrick's larking around at mealtimes. The lesson of a teacher who scrimps and scrapes when it comes to humour, or worse, straight-laced and blind-eyed, directs a Nelson telescope towards the pupils' free and fast-moving, teetering-on-the-brink fantasy (*wherever* that may irreverently be directed!), is not likely to go like a house on fire.

Betty Staley in her commendable study *Between Form and Freedom* has shared an enormous amount of her experience of the adolescent. On the back of that, fantasy may be seen as the element which prevents form from stagnating, while ensuring that freedom is wisely contained. It can *inform freedom* and *save form from dying* into the checklist or the rampant claw of the inspectorate. Even the expensive teeth behind the benign smile of today's mentor-, assessor-, evaluator-, adviser-, consultant-, public enquiry-, investigator-, counsellor-culture might be worth looking out for. This is by no means to deny accountability, transparency and responsibility as Steiner clearly and continuously stresses.

Thus, while there is much in the teacher that must resemble the stability of a castle on a rock, the portcullis must be raised from time to time to admit the fresh air of fantasy to blow away the dust-gathering cobwebs, stir any staleness that is residual from the kind of textbooks or unincinerated handbooks the teacher has been obliged to use in preparation, and flap the well-worn clothes of the past into jocular, Windsor-Castle-on-Washing-Day, *creatively-on-line pedagogy* and lesson-enlivening freshness.

UPPER SCHOOL

The Wider Significance of the Arts

'Can we say this?'

Such a thing had never happened before. A pupil called out after we had worked a little at the poem we were saying as a choral recitation first thing in the morning. Having burnished a phrase here, timed a dramatic pause there, and adjusted the tone of a crescendo somewhere else, we finally said it all through. Not with any intention, I might add, of the class getting a taste of 'performing' it at a school function. But evidently one person in the class had felt that it was ready, or soon would be, for public consumption. The incident sticks in the memory not only because it was unique, but because the pupil in question had hitherto had nothing to say in those parts of the main-lesson that were open to discussion, let alone being incisive in such a taking-the-bull-by-the-horns manner. And it was not as if the class was somewhere in the middle of the Lower School, ebullient with natural childhood spontaneity. This was Class 9 where one might reasonably have expected more belligerence than bubbling enthusiasm.

The incident almost eclipses other relevant details. It was a main-lesson in modern history and I was attempting to give the class a feeling for the enormous stride forward that the French contribution to Western civilization had made in the seventeenth century essentially (culminating in the Baroque), followed by the lost potential of the French Revolution—its banner for the future, of Liberty, Equality and Fraternity, having gone the bloody way it did—and Napoleon's inserting his military genius into the ensuing social maelstrom, finally (as Beethoven perceived when he struck out the name of Napoleon from the dedication of the title page of the *Eroica Symphony*) endangering the foreward progress of Europe with the threat of French domination of a kind that harked back to a past social order.

There is more to it than that, of course, but here I am limiting myself to a summary of the background from which the poem we were learning sprang. It was Charles Wolfe's *The Burial of Sir John Moore after Corunna*, a poem that I had heard recommended by Eileen Hutchins (founder of the Elmfield Steiner School in Stourbridge) for its adolescent appeal, its vivid, epic-like imagery and its dramatic rhythm.

The class had proved her judgement to be pedagogically sound, if proof were needed. It had taken to the poem from the outset, and daily we explored consonantal sequences, the 'melody' of each line, short and long vowels, the poet's choice of vocabulary, etc. They relished these elements consciously and were beginning to put heart and soul into their speech. The spirit of language came alive, a moving experience at any time, but especially so when those who give it breath are a group (gaggle, crowd, phalanx, bunch … oh for a prize collective noun that would do it justice!) of young adolescents. Why is this so? One of the main reasons for not addressing the awakening dimension of a child's consciousness before adolescence goes back to Steiner's recommendation that *the awakening should take place in 'richness of soul'*.

The Lower School and the Early Years are about endowing the soul with that richness. It is as though the naturally awakening intellect then has capital from which it can draw to invest in its own exploration, the intellectual explorations thereupon yielding further riches for the soul. Problems only arise if the intellect is 'underfunded'. Barrenness, illusion, indiscrimination, skimming the surface, easily influenced distortion, naively succumbing to the latest 'ology', theory at odds with the actual phenomena, the mind in an ivory tower are amongst the dangers that can ensue.

Thus, when the pupil steps from Lower School to Upper School, from Class 8 to Class 9, the pedagogy changes gear, as it were, to acknowledge the passage from pure enrichment to striving awakening. Consequently, when the geology teacher speaks about Carboniferous or Silurian times, the pupil will have already 'met' the respective rocks (through descriptions, excursions, handling the actual minerals but *not through chemical formulae*), and their associated topography. The process is akin to the kind of experience one has when an acquaintance reveals something of the background to some climacteric moment in their biography: why they moved house; how they came to change jobs; what enabled them to visit the Far East; some remark in a book they read which was at the root of their changing aspects of their lifestyle; a seemingly chance meeting—while waiting in a bus station queue or when buying an umbrella—which opened up new avenues of thought and led to the world outlook that largely now informs their life; and so on.

That pedagogical step seems fairly clear in subjects such as geology, embryology, psychology, botany, astronomy, and in history and geography too. But where does it leave the *arts*? To only *understand* art is to miss the point. What rhythm is the poet using? What key is the composer modulating to? What mathematical proportions did the builders incorporate in the great Gothic cathedrals? What material did Leonardo use in painting his frescoes? It may well be significant to understand what is going on, but unless the full impact of the artist's creation comes across, something will be missing.

Steiner regarded that 'something' as an important consideration in teaching the adolescent. In general, art (both performing and visual) up to Class 7 has been part and parcel of their childhood educational experience. Alongside basic exercises, warehouses *of repertoire* will have been stocked in music and poetry and eurythmy. Memory holds the key to those warehouses: broadly speaking, of music in the soul, of poetry in the mind and heart, of eurythmy in the whole body. And the visual arts (drawing, painting, modelling) will have provided the teacher with the means of *deepening the pupil's experience* of most subjects. To arrive at these two points, however, will also have required introducing media, techniques and artistic 'laws', *all in appropriately pedagogical ways*.

The Upper School makes new demands. In their awakening soul condition, the young people become increasingly conscious of those elements in each art which the artist employs, and which contribute to making the art aesthetically *effective*. Questions/issues will be explored such as: How has the poet used alliteration to aesthetic effect? What is the effect of periodically breaking the regularity within the iambic pentameter? The effect of a short, pregnant line at the end of a verse? A flowing hexameter? A breathlessly hastening anapaest? The repetition of an opening line in a phrase? Extended parentheses? Synecdoche and other figures of speech? Similar questions relevant to the other arts are explored in the same spirit of enquiry. The value of poetry in a school framework, over and above the other arts—though this is not to claim that it stands on an artistic pinnacle of some kind—is that (a) no media have to be first mastered, and every pupil can speak (and poetry is the art of the *spoken word*); (b) considerable aesthetic ground can be covered in a comparatively short time (compare the time it takes to speak the few verses of a Shelley ode with the hours spent—however well—on reading a lengthy Dickens or Dostoevsky novel, for instance); and (c) though speaking in *chorus*, the individual can completely personalize the experience (cf. the totally different dimension to experiencing a Chopin prelude for pianoforte, a masque by Ben Jonson, a large-scale collage, or even the drawing of a simple pastel).

Steiner goes on to make clear the role of these enhanced artistic experiences in the life of the students in their third seven-year period. The kind of thinking that we associate with our day-wake consciousness is in the first place causal. We think of cause and effect, origins and consequences. We ask: Is it plausible? Does it stand up to logical scrutiny? Is it reasonable? But in many existential questions—the life after death is an example that has engaged humanity from time immemorial—we come up against uncrossable boundaries if we remain stuck in purely logical (brain-bound?) thinking. Therefore, *as a balance*, alongside focusing the wakening intellect on aspects of knowledge acquired, e.g. via emotional intelligence in the earlier years, the adolescent needs richness of experience that is not confined to plausibility. The creative exploration of the arts provides this balance. The arts complement the left-brained pursuit of knowledge, but they also have to measure up to the adolescent's growing awareness, increasing self-respect, advancing self-objectivity. A slovenly or superficial performance of a play or orchestral piece will be embarrassingly at odds with the adolescent's 'standards'—at least as far as they are publicly witnessed. But whether performed or exhibited or not, the uncovering of the aesthetic validity of each artistic creation is what will add right-brain weight to the balance.

The poem about the burial of Sir John Moore had, on that memorable morning, moved from simmering on the artistic back burner to coming up to the boil—hence the incisive remark, 'Can we say this?' The tone of voice was less of a rhetorical question and more of a thoroughly convinced: We jolly well should. Amidst the horseplay and lethargy, the emotional upheaval and will-deserted doldrums of adolescence, it is not always easy to bring artistic endeavours 'up to the boil'. So this is another strand in the 'art of education' that needs methodically spinning, but it is nonetheless an essential ingredient in the fabric of these challenging years, challenging for both teacher and pupil. From this point of view, an education which fails to do full justice to the arts is, at one stroke, halving its long-term value to the pupil. Though the quietest pupil in the class blurting out 'Can we say this?' is one chance in a million, the full inner stature of *each* human being in adolescence is silently yet imploringly shaking the educationist by the shoulders with the sentiment from which it is drafted.

Universality

'My lord, I come your daughter's hand/ In bedlock fair to seek!'

It was a play I'd written for Class 1 based on a French fairy story 'The Mouse Princess'. The theme, in essence, concerns that aspect of human life which seeks to avoid extremes and pursue a *middle path*. This necessitates the oft-recurrent motif in such tales, not only from France, of threefoldness: *a polarity with a mean*. The images in the story are taken from spinning and weaving. The too-earthly inclined soul produces a yarn that is too thick, almost knotted and unyielding, and a cloth that is so ruthlessly beaten during the weaving that it more or less stands up on end of its own accord. The too-spiritually inclined soul's yarn is far too thin and given to snapping at the slightest provocation, while the length of cloth is so loosely woven and uneven that it resembles a fishing net in places. (Had it been made up into a dress, modesty would certainly have disapproved, though hardly anything of that sort in today's fashion arena gets rejected.) The perfect yarn (fine but strong), and the perfect cloth (delicate but substantial) are produced by a princess who has been enchanted into a mouse. So the whole 'plot' offers plenty of food for fun.

There are three princes, of course. They are bidden by the king, their ageing father, to find suitable wives. Suitability is imaged in this instance not by wealth but by the extent to which the ladies they are wooing are incarnated right into their yarn-spinning, cloth-weaving, dressmaking fingertips— a remarkable image of the soul (a feminine element in each person's makeup) cultivating her forces of thinking (q.v. thread of thought), feeling (the warp and weft of self-consciousness and a sensitive empathy towards the other person), and willing (the garment of our actions that we show the world). The one who inherits the kingdom is the prince whose wife to be (the image of the soul) has cultivated her forces so that the ego (a masculine principle in each one of us) is potentially able to confer upon the soul the crown of 'higher worlds'.

It was in the midst of rehearsing all this that the little prince (a somewhat squat, magnificently dreamy, fair-haired phlegmatic boy) pursuing the too-spiritually inclined count's daughter, came out with his unconsciously edited version of the text, *changing wedlock to bedlock* (tacet Freud!). The fun seemed to be veering towards the crater's edge of getting out of hand, but only for the astonished teacher. No one else in the class of some two dozen batted an eyelid. It's now 30 years later; I wonder as I write whether a slip of the tongue of that order, with today's precocious 7-year-olds, would escape equally unnoticed!

Apart from a main-lesson going thoroughly into embryology, usually in Class 10, Steiner referred comparatively little to sexuality in the context of education. His main concern, it would appear, was on the one hand, that the awaking consciousness of the adolescent should not be trapped into an absorbing concern with the maturing physical body to the extent that wider horizons should be obliterated by what he termed *eroticism*. The place of the arts in keeping open the view towards these wider horizons has been discussed in a previous chapter. On the other hand, in recognizing that with the maturation of the physical body, of which the attraction towards those of the opposite gender was the natural consequence, Steiner was deeply concerned that the adolescent's propensity for love—the bud of love of the young child for family and those in the immediate circle swelling into blossom as family and other close social boundaries give way and expand towards the wider community—should be greatly encouraged but directed towards *universality*. Humanity as a whole is where this naturally born powerful force should be directed rather than exclusively funnelled into the narrow confines of love (if that's what it is) that finds a form of self-satisfaction in the sexuality of the physical body.

Today, no one is squeamish about a subject whose taboo disappeared when birds and bees started being poisoned through what was happenng to the the food chain. In Steiner's day things were different. Yet he was emphatic about the co-educational aspect of the Waldorf School. Why shouldn't boys and girls do gym together? Every child should knit. Gender was simply not an issue. His innovative ideas were not merely to do with what we now think of as women's lib, thus also having no problem with the equal opportunities of men and women on the staff. At the same time there was not the confusion that we have fallen into between masculine and male, and between feminine and female, whereby vital qualities that the two sexes contribute to society as a whole are blurred and therefore are in danger of being lost. Indeed, Steiner went out of his way to characterize and explain the pedagogy suited to boy and girl in adolescence.

A particularly helpful ingredient in education, for expanding the younger person's capacity towards universal love, is the main-lesson on ancient history. This may sound a bit far-fetched to say the least! After two years devoted to modern history (Class 8 and 9), in which the young person can find parallels with their own state of pubescent turmoil, it is refreshing and liberating to suddenly go far away to where the receding tides of time are gradually revealing more and more archaeological insights into history. Such concerns begin to cultivate a sense of objectivity—often the last thing one associates with the emotional oscillations of adolescence. Nevertheless, objectivity, and the partial or temporary control (eradication would be going too far) of egotistic self-seeking, is clearly a (*the?*) prerequisite for the engendering of universal love. Any Westerner who has cringed at the culture shock experienced in travelling through Lima, Bombay, Mexico City, Ramalla, Lagos, Soweto, and such places will have experienced something of his own shortcomings in regard to unconditional, universal love. Perhaps one of the few people who got so far was Francis of Assisi—one could cite more recent examples. One must remember, however, that among other components of adolescence is the birth of *idealism*. Most of us go over the top at some point regarding this, with illusions about changing the world. Without idealism, however, how would the adolescent avoid falling into the materialistic rut of getting a 'good' (safe, well-paid) job, sticking to and continuing along old, well-worn tracks which do not require any initiative, becoming one of the 'sport' hooligans who bring whatever game they support into disrepute, and ... and ....

The idealist in the adolescent needs to experience how ancient cultures conducted life if he or she is going to contribute effectively to the metamorphosis of what was cold war, the present grid-locked world economy, the religious fundamentalism stalemating so much of modern culture, and so on.

The first Waldorf School opened its doors partially in response to the aftermath of the 1914–18 World War. With society in tatters, male populations utterly depleted, vast swathes of the countryside devastated, towns in ruins, economics on the brink of disaster, the bloated hopes of imperialism punctured, morale and morals sliding downhill, international politics moving inexorably towards yet another war, it was the workforce of the Waldorf Astoria cigarette factory, and one of their directors, Dr Emil Molt, who considered that the future could not be built simply by reinstating the past. New forces were needed. These could come from nowhere except from within the human being. Waldorf education seeks to engender such forces. But though it arose from Steiner's world outlook, spiritual science or anthroposophy, the education does not seek to imbue the pupils with that outlook. It would not achieve universality that way. Nevertheless, anthroposophical activities have nothing to hide and occasionally the spotlight will fall on one or the other. The following chapter cites an instance when this happened.

Choosing a Path in the Light of Self-identity

'OK, Mr Masters! The game's up; we admit it!'

It was towards the end of a botany main-lesson in Class 11. Being more of a nature lover (if I'm honest) than a natural scientist, I had chosen as authentic a route as I could think of, following the plan of a book entitled *The Plant (Die Pflanze)*, which had been written by the botanist who taught at the Waldorf School in Rudolf Steiner's day.

There is a spicy story attached to how this individual, Grohmann, became a member of the Anthroposophical Society. As a student in Vienna, he'd heard of spiritual science and, as every good student well might be, was very wary. At first sight, it seemed nonsense that anyone could speak of anything to do with the spirit in the same breath as *science*. However, as open-mindedness should surely be an absolute for the scientist, he thought he'd give it a go, and so planned to go to a lecture being given by Rudolf Steiner. Steiner drew large audiences, so he would be able to sit there perfectly anonymously. It is related that he went with a friend, but that their spirit of enquiry was not untainted with cynicism and that the cynicism had a mischievous twist in it. The pair of them combed the encyclopaedia for a plant they had never come across anywhere else, either in reference books or in their botany lectures. It happened to be in the rain forests of the Amazon. They had heard that at the end of his lectures, Steiner frequently addressed questions, the procedure being that the questions were handed to him written on slips of paper. Their strategy was to ask what spiritual science had to say about the remote and well-nigh unknown plant. (I have always imagined that they couldn't within reason have expected a direct answer, but that they would judge 'spiritual science' by the *way* in which Rudolf Steiner—the initiate of the modern age—admitted that this was an area which had not been researched by spiritual science.)

As expected, when the lecture was over, questions were handed up to the rostrum, and Steiner read out the first one. One wonders whether their suspense allowed them much spare attentiveness for the answers he gave. When he came to their paper he put it on one side, on the table beside which he stood. It was actually not the only question that received this treatment. However, he eventually took up the pile that had been sifted through in this way—and here the anecdote must surely have gained some apocryphal embroidery—and repeated the sifting process several times, so that the suspense must have been considerably compounded. Would he address the question, or leave the paper completely discarded? Finally theirs was the only piece of paper left. Steiner took it up and read out the question: 'What can spiritual science say about ...?' After remaining deep in thought for some moments, in answer he first gave two or three pieces of factual information, on the assumption that most of the audience would not have heard of the plant(!)—one wonders whether he had to resist commenting, in good-humoured response, on the question's unique irrelevance to the lecture that had just been given!—and then added that what was not generally known (except to local tribesmen) was the plant's medicinal properties. With thanks to their lucky stars, I suppose, and the triumph of open-mindedness over cynicism, the two students became members of the Society on the spot, and Grohmann became the one who pioneered the Waldorf approach to botany, presumably with a soft spot for every mischievous pupil who turned up in class!

As part of the main-lesson I am describing—albeit interruptedly—it was more a case of a mischievous teacher! Let me explain. I had always been on my guard against off-loading undigested anthroposophy onto 'minors'. This was mainly a matter of steering mealtime conversation well clear of anything that could be labelled by discerning adolescents as 'Steinerized'. There were the occasional direct questions, of course, but these were very few and far between, and apart from having to deal with visitors invited to meals, who didn't follow the same code of conduct, our long-suffering family only (*only!*) had to contend with the lifestyle.

The crunch came at school however. How could one make pupils aware of the vistas that had been opened up by spiritual-scientific research and yet totally avoid any trace of proselytizing, worse still, conditioning? With the vast benefits to the health of human beings and to the restoration of earth fertility that biodynamic agriculture had achieved, I felt duty bound in the main-lesson to include some aspects of it in order to understand the forces at work in the plant, with the intention of showing how the empirically substantiated results (no BSE in cattle, for instance on biodynamic farms) spoke for themselves.

I took my lead from a drawing of Goethe's. The Hawaiian University Press had brought out a translation of his writings on botany and the publication included a drawing of a tulip, one of whose petals had appeared lower down the stem than the rest. Goethe had picked up the fact—his powers of observation being outstanding—that the petal's form veered towards that of a leaf, which led him to the concept of the metamorphosis of forces in the plant: leaf to blossom, blossom to fruit/seed. Having looked at the process of growth in the plant with the class, from germination (with radical and cotyledon as primitive plant organs) through to self-reproduction via the seed, I turned the class's attention first to some current problems.

A firm in Sri Lanka had persuaded many local rice growers

to switch from their traditional, indigenous varieties to the firm's highly developed 'wonder' variety. Too late, the farmers discovered that the seed from the rice they kept aside for next year's sowing didn't germinate. We tried in class to grasp what was happening: the added yield, an increase in *substance,* had been at at the expense of *vitality.* Fortunately, someone on foreseeing the dilemma that would ensue, had created a seed bank, collecting local Sri Lankan strains of rice and growing them year in, year out just so that they would not be lost.

We next looked at kindred phenomena to the *fall* of vitality into substance. Examples were: the nodal arrangement of leaves normally found on the stem of a plant, brought down below ground in the case of the potato (its so-called eyes); the stamens of the carnation were 'reduced' to formless petals (formless compared with the petals of the wild *Dianthus* from which the carnation has been developed); the occasional tomato that is not round like its neighbours but displays a protuberance on one side, reminiscent of a lower plant organ—such specimens don't get to market! And there was, of course, Goethe's prime example, the 'fallen' tulip petal. Thus if there is evidence that the plant can fail (even if only in part) to transform its forces of life upwards, it is reasonable to suppose that in other cases the dynamic upsurge of its forces *is* taking place as part of nature's bounty. At this point, I slipped in the concept of something *dynamic* happening, and I felt gradually confident that the pupils were with me.

Here, I have a confession to make. I have deliberately misquoted the speaker at the head of the chapter and slightly misled the reader. For it was at this point in the lesson that one of the boys (aged 17)—an East Ender if I remember rightly, very down to earth, clumping into class each morning in his motorcycle gear, looking like something from

Mars—said *not what I have headed the chapter with* (though I do believe that that expressed what the twinkle in his eye was communicating) but: 'OK Mr Masters, tell us what bio-dynamic agriculture is.' For me it was a moment of quiet exhilaration. *His* thinking, albeit prompted, had freely and open-mindedly overcome any residual prejudice from his emotional adolescent days and his scorn for Steinerisms.

The 17-year-old's emergence from the vale of adolescence towards the heights of adulthood (though let us not pretend they are giddy heights) brings with it an earnest search for a personal stance. The heights lend overview, from which the incoming individuality can determine its perspective.

Thus the task of the teacher of 17-year-olds is to strengthen the independence of thought and judgement as a basis for taking responsibility, lift the clouds which are obscuring overview and offer some perspectives so that the incoming individuality realizes that there is choice when it comes to world outlooks and that *self-determination of the individual* is something that can be consciously cultivated.

Of course, on that school morning, I also had to admit that the game was up—my pedagogical game. Yet it was not a game in the sense of trickery. The vibrancy of pedagogy comes out in what is *at play*. The more prescriptive a cur-riculum, the less room will there be for play. No wonder Steiner gave the curriculum so little prominence in his (albeit unspelled-out) theory of education, bordering in fact on the irrelevant—'If there is no teacher to teach a subject, it's better to omit it [better than to teach it badly, i.e. with inadequate pedagogical play].'

Stepping into Life

'You're a friend of ours, aren't you?'

It was early December. As I walked to school, excitement trembled in the air. The Advent Fair had taken place at the weekend and the build-up to Christmas with wreaths, transparencies, Advent calendars, carols and other traditions was under way. The previous evening had been a new experience for me. A small, but exceptionally well-run school hostel was celebrating St Nicholas—in the good old Dutch tradition of singling out members of the community one by one with 'messages' which purported to work in such a way that they improved the behaviour of the person to whom they were directed. Like star-script of some kind, St Nicholas carried a book, an impressive, weighty tome in every sense of the word. On one side of each double page were the 'golden entries', things to commend in each child's behaviour; opposite—and the reader may ponder what colour they would choose to have opposite to gold—were the negative entries. The colleagues who ran the hostel had invited me to carry that book—to be St Nicholas.

The pedagogical skill of the occasion was to draw attention to a person's peccadilloes in such a way that the resolve to correction was awoken *from within*. I had been chosen, it transpired, because it had got around that I had written poetry, though it was before the days when I began publishing: 'It's the poet in you [that we need on this occasion],' was how it came over in the briefing session which took place some evenings before, when St Nicholas was measured to ensure his costume would fit and was given some insight into the behavioural characteristics (golden or otherwise) of those concerned. At school we always held this ceremony on or as close as possible to 6 December, St Nicholas' Day itself, but only for Classes 1–3, where the dream consciousness of make-believe could still be involved. I was therefore surprised at the 'candidates' for St Nicholas's remark-accompanied gifts. The hostel had pupils right up to Class 12, far, far beyond the stage of dream consciousness, and St Nicholas was expected to have the appropriate psychological tact to address anyone within that range.

The 'magic' of the occasion in some mysterious way already descended for me (the mantel of St Nicholas?) as I walked in the early fading light of sunset to the hostel—I had decided to dispense with reindeer and go on foot, despite it necessitating covering a tract of roadless countryside that was unfamiliar to me. Nature in any case seems at its lowest ebb in November and December. The lonely chirrup of a bird or two as night fell and the hoot of an owl served to enhance the hush-hush that surrounded the event. It was essential for the younger children that, behind the copious white beard and beneath the majestic wine-red mitre, the person be totally incognito so that the child's fantasy had uninhibited room for play, in which this exhortation 'from another world' had the optimum chance of making the right impression and of working positively. It was a great tribute to the hostel parents that they had nurtured the atmosphere in which this special opportunity of the year could work.

What with that, meeting on some higher plane—for such it seemed—the candlelit room where the event took place, followed afterwards by the long walk home in pitch darkness, I was still in something of a reverie the morning after as I made my way to main-lesson.

Winding one's way through the playground and the games of tag, which were already nimbly taking place even at this time of day, was always accompanied by a few morning greetings. But that morning held a surprise greeting—a strange, totally unexpected inner something. A Class 12 pupil, whom I had never taught and hardly knew except by name, stepped out from the milling crowd and gazed at me with an indescribable expression (a mixture of peace, quiet happiness, positive resignation and what seemed like universal love). In a flash I recognized that she must have been present the evening before. As I hardly checked my step, all she said was: 'You're a friend of ours, aren't you Mr Masters?' The poise, the balance, the maturity, the soul-weight, the acknowledgement 'we are fellow human beings', the readiness to shoulder life, and all in ten seconds, still echo on— although I do not recall ever speaking to her again. That moment still somehow remains one of life's significant encounters. It was like, I imagine, though I don't wish to exaggerate—I am merely fishing for words—coming across a sign of life, a fellow traveller, in a barren tract of land, or a desert stranger, some sort of godsend at a dire moment when one needs a helping hand.

Every summer there is a lot of talk, media-driven, about A levels. Higher education fiends ensure that we continually respect, preferably aspire to, the various levels that each rung of the ladder represents, up to the acme of doctorate (level 8). There is no doubt value somewhere in all that. But what is of inestimably greater value is the level which one hopes to achieve by Class 12 in a Waldorf school: that of inner strength, inner ability, empathy, self-knowledge, growing awareness of the *meaning of life*. All that has gone before forms the basis, of course, of cutting and polishing the twelfth jewel that is to take its place in the crown of manhood or womanhood. The work of this 12th year—studies in philosophy, comparative world religions, styles in the architecture that humanity has created to give dwelling-places to its dead, its parliaments, its sacraments, its airports, its hospitals, its astronomical observatories, its theatres, its domestic habitations, and so on, together with sciences, handicrafts, performing and visual arts—helps each student to arrive at the standpoint they personally need.

Once, on a visit to the Waldorf School in Cali, Colombia, I was invited to meet with their Class 12. One of the students translated the conversation. The pupils greeted me with warm friendliness; it was rare for them to meet a European. Colombia isn't sought after by tourists as are the beaches of Florida or ancient sites such as the great amphitheatre at Epidaurus in Greece or the colossal stone circle at Stonehenge on the Wiltshire plains. After some friendly exchanges they wanted to know how Colombians are viewed in Europe. They were clearly concerned lest the rest of the world should have a one-sided, possibly bigoted view of their country as being nothing but a reflection of anarchical drug trafficking cartels. There was a wonderful blend of innocence and maturity in these 18-year-olds, which no doubt owes something to the ethnic setting in which they had been raised, but which was undoubtedly also a product of their Waldorf education. I was amazed when, during the same week, they one day took out their recorders to play to me. Consider it: some 30 18-year-olds—*Latin-American* 18-year-olds—playing descant recorders! With devotion and concentrated seriousness, they played a theme from a Tchaikovsky symphony, managing somehow, with that unavoidably thin, high-pitched sound, to experience at least the essence of Romanticism in music, if not the voluptuously full-blooded impact with which it can sweep you off your feet if played by the Moscow Philharmonic. Those Colombians used what they'd got to make a meaningful step towards what they intended to become.

Perhaps the most symptomatic aid to maturation at this age is to be found in the approach to history. From Class 5 to Class 8 the pupils have been taken through a chronological journey in which they have met the great figures on the stage of history and the results of their actions. *Par excellence*, these are the stories of history. In the Upper School, these events are trawled over once more from the point of view of cause and effect. This experience tallies with the pupils' emerging penchant, indeed hunger, for rationality. At the same time, there will be many unanswered questions. With history, one often feels like the 4-year-old with his endless whining: Why? You are tempted into answering a tad too intellectually and back it comes: Why? *Fable convenu* so often keeps the lid firmly shut on history (What is dark about the Middle Ages?), ignores enigmas (Why did a dyed-in-the-blood republican like Garibaldi countenance the enthronement of Victor Emanuel as king of the liberated Italy?), misrepresents the facts (What was the real consequence of the Allies burdening Germany with so much of the war guilt of the 1914–18 War?), presents a biased view (Why do we place so little emphasis on Henry VIII's first marriage and gloat over his subsequent marital behaviour?), dresses the facts in national pride (What country is not guilty of this?), and so on. Steiner therefore recommended that these masks be torn away as far as possible in Class 12 and that one come—and it is the third time that one is looking at the facts—to a deeper, truer and more revealing understanding of history, even if one cannot always get completely to the bottom of it.

Wrestling with such streams that sometimes throw up their deeper currents onto the surface of human life is of enormous benefit to the spirit of enquiry that one is hoping to instil in the 18-year-old. If a pupil attends a Waldorf school for all twelve classes, it would be fair to say that at least for those years his or her footsteps are outwardly more of less foreordained. But the paths leading to further destiny are likely to take the individual through steep, life-challenging experiences, experiences which reach to the human spirit's deepest foundations. If education has supported those foundations in becoming dependable, it will have contributed something invaluable to life. The path may quake, but the spirit will hold fast.

Such an educational aim manifestly cannot be represented by lists of achievements in the school mag—and in any case, children are more aware of who is 'a friend of ours' amongst the adults who surround and nurture them than the aims by which those adults guide their vocation. Of course, the achievements count, very much so. But the stream of life not only consists of the play of light on its rippling surface and the spray with which it spatters the boulders that jut out at its side; its course depends on the bedrock of the valley through which it flows.

OUTLOOK

A Final Comment: The Public Eye

'You'll avoid those esoteric references, I'm sure.'

I had been asked to speak at a divorce proceding, a sad case it has to be said—in which one parent earnestly wanted the children to continue attending their Steiner school and the other didn't. My task essentially was to refute the allegations that the education did not prepare children sufficiently for life. At the time, I was doing my ten-year stint for the Steiner Schools Fellowship as Chair, and assignments that needed someone whose office in itself carried weight often took me, as in this case, to places that could be broadly characterized as 'shop window'. A court of law, of course, is looking more deeply into the case than what is shown in window dressing, and I had come ready with philosophical and educational broadsides should they be called for.

The parent who was in favour of continuing with the education won the case and was both relieved and elated, but the point I want to make here concerns the briefing. This was double-barrelled: first the solicitor who had prepared the case went through her checklist with me; then I had a relaxed but insightful time with the barrister. It was the latter who alerted me to how the man in the street (which in this case included *the man on the bench*) viewed Steiner's remarkable approach to educational matters.

She had obviously done a considerable amount of background reading, and highlighted in the conversation points she thought would be supportive. But in a somewhat parenthetical yet decidedly precise way—extremely British I remember thinking—she inserted what clearly was a concern. Goodness knows how deeply she had gone in her reading, but the worry she had was what she referred to as

Steiner's *esoteric references*. Had that been all she'd said, my mind might have raced in the direction of the spiritual hierarchies where Steiner makes links with the School of Athens and the teachings of St Paul, or the cosmic forces at work in certain biodynamic agricultural preparations made in order to increase soil fertility and the nutritional value in plants, or in a dozen and one other directions which even a cursory glance at the edition of Steiner's complete works (over 300 volumes) might suggest. But it was none of this. It was the frequent allusion Steiner makes in his educational lectures to the eruption in childhood of the second dentition and its relevance for the passing from informal to formal education. As we saw, this is connected to the working of the etheric organization, and at this the barrister either felt out of her depth or, to give her the benefit of the doubt, was simply convinced that such a topic would go down in the eyes of the court like a lead balloon.

What amused me was the way the solicitor had reacted to the same dimension of Steiner's concept of child development. 'Steer clear of those crazy bits about the second teeth,' was her bull-at-a-gate—rather cockney, unless my ears deceived me—way of putting it. In fact, if she hadn't been so direct, I'm not sure that I would have fully cottoned on to what the barrister meant by avoiding those 'esoteric references'. With mild amusement, I thought back to the hosts of children I'd known with their wobbly front teeth, and tooth-gapped grins, finding the memory about as down-to-earth— decidedly *not* esoteric—as anything I could think of. But let that pass: (a) there wasn't time to comment, as we were already walking towards the courtroom when the remark was made ('At least, whatever else happens, he'll remember my last instruction,' I could imagine her thinking); and (b) the point was not the *what* but rather the *how* this aspect of Steiner's intense and far-reaching research into the nature of the growing child was seen by superficial eyes—though I am not in the least suggesting that there was any trace of derision in the superficiality.

How Waldorf education is seen publicly can be taken, I would suggest, as a kind of barometer that reveals the degree of materialism in the politico-social arena at any given place, at any given time. The Nazi closure of Waldorf schools in the 30s is as indicative as is the respect and support that the German State rapidly accorded the education soon after the Second World War. Clearly, the philosophically coherent approach that Waldorf represents is something that cultural German thinking can encompass, appreciate and respect.

How different it has been in the UK. At the same time as the above court case, there was a move in the UK to get Waldorf a place on the political map, which would be advantageous to parents who chose the education for their children and who could reasonably hope for their rights to make that choice to be financially acknowledged by the government in accordance with the United Nations Universal Declaration of Human Rights of 10 February 1948. Statements of support for the education were made both in the House of Lords and at the committee stage of the Bill in the House of Commons (as on record in *Hansard*). With my official role at the time, I was deeply involved in both procedures.

The political measure that was eventually used to *prevent* official recognition of and financial support for the education need not be gone into here. Though disappointed, I was not surprised. One of the protagonists who had gone out of her way, with whole-hearted generosity, to ensure we 'met the right people', remarked when our expectations began to look doubtful and the outcome bleak, 'You'll never get recognition with this ethic!' Similar warning signs had been heard when a group in Brighton had applied to establish a City

Technology College under the Thatcherite government. Their efforts were exemplary and they got as far as acquiring a building. The then Secretary of State for Education, however, on realizing the integrity of Waldorf education, was reported to have remarked in a less guarded moment, '*We'll* have to cover our a . . . s'! This, of course, was not the reason given for the College's demise!

During the intervening decade, governments across the world have given support to Waldorf education in one way or another while the movement in the UK treads water— *treads it very actively* though, through the appointment of a professional political lobbyist (with considerable consequences for the Fellowship's budget). The recent press release announcing the go ahead for the feasibility study concerning the Hereford Waldorf School, which could lead to government funding, is a tribute to her lobbying skills.

In September 2004 there were plans in the United States to give vouchers to 1799 students to attend private schools (this is only a fraction of the 65,000 who were deemed to be at 'low performing' State schools). This was at least an attempt to jump-start the school voucher idea, which is not quite as old as the hills but certainly one that political parties over the last decades have dangled carrot-enticingly before the voters, though with very limited success.

The deep concern in the UK is the cost of the voucher or its political equivalent. That is obviously a major obstacle in a country with a centuries-long 'public' school tradition, where vouchers for all school ages would mean a fairly hefty extra item of public expenditure. The possible incursion into the ethics of Waldorf is what worries the practitioner. The ominous adage 'He who pays the piper calls the tune' warns that a partnership would not necessarily harmonize with the 'unshakeables' of Waldorf, and the last thing that would benefit Waldorf would be a situation similar to that in the

State sector where gifted teachers quit because bureaucratic regulations forcibly and consistently prevent their creativity. Steiner's view of education depends, amongst other factors which we have discussed, on the creative exertion of each individual teacher. Its integrity is due to that, as has been its success, and its educational (as opposed to administrative) failures could be said to have been due to the lack of it.

One is tempted to acknowledge that those with misgivings who say, 'Better no Waldorf than one in which the ethic is diluted, diverted, misrepresented or contaminated,' have a point. Taking a more optimistic view, however, everything is likely to depend on the future generation's ability to create a *language* (based on sound research) that is able to present all those 'bits about the second teeth', which are so fundamental to Steiner, without their coming across as 'crazy', while at the same time the esoteric spark remains alive in the Waldorf teacher's praxis as much as in their inner integrity. If Waldorf can be achieved in those respects, and the piper's accountability can be suitably demonstrated, he who pays the piper may well develop the interest and wisdom not to call a piper's tune that might sound discordant beside the maxims to which the piper subscribes, but to *listen* to the tune that the one with the pipe at his experienced lips is versatile at playing. That, I firmly believe, will be to the benefit of all concerned. It is surely a lesson that has not only been learnt in Germany, the country which mothered Waldorf in the first place, as well as other countries beyond the shores of the UK, but one which has implications for the future of education in general.

To divorce Waldorf from its maxims would be a triumph for the forces of destruction. At the same time there continues to be much work to be done to present the 'crazy bits about the second teeth'—and all the rest of those 'esoteric references'—with sobriety and conviction, and in a way that is not only accessible to the modern mind but is in full accord with those who have the best interests of the future of humanity at heart *and in their searching minds.*

Index